Neil Forsyth is an author and journalist. A fellow Dundonian and friend to Bob Servant for over twenty years, he has recently completed Servant's biography, *Bob Servant: Hero of Dundee*, also available from Birlinn. Forsyth is also author of *Other People's Money*, the biography of fraudster Elliot Castro, and a novel, *Let Them Come Through*.

Praise for *Delete This At Your Peril*

'*Delete This at Your Peril* is a very, very funny book and a perfect present for anybody who has: A) a sense of humour and B) gets irritated by Internet spammers and their tiresome scams . . . You will piss yourself and then quote sections of this book repeatedly within your circle of friends'
Irvine Welsh

'Incredibly funny'
Jimmy Boyle, author of *A Sense of Freedom*

'Hilarious. I laughed so much I nearly gave him my account number'
Martin Kelner, The Guardian

'Reminds me how good good comic writing can be . . . The surrealism is perfect'
Scotland on Sunday

'*Delete This at Your Peril* carries the spoof letter genre into the internet age . . . A former cheeseburger magnate and semi-retired window cleaner, Bob is a delightfully deranged but likeable rogue. Drinking in and chasing 'skirt' around the bars of Broughty Ferry with ne'er-do-well mates such as Frank The Plank, he is a late-middle-aged working-class eccentric in the vein of John Shuttleworth . . . a living, breathing creation of comic genius . . . Today Broughty Ferry. Tomorrow, the world?'
Bookbag

'He's a Henry Root for the digital age . . . a hilarious collection'
GT Magazine

'Hurrah for Bob Servant! He wreaks revenge on the fraudsters, making them dance to his tune with his wonderfully surreal replies. Read it in private as it will make you laugh out lou
really couldn't happen to a nicer bunch
The Book Magazine

'Bob neatly turns the tables, leaving a trail of comic carnage as he gradually draws the unsuspecting crooks into his own outlandish schemes . . . eminently readable and absurdly funny'
Cherwell

'Genius! Highly entertaining and brilliantly deranged'
Maxim

'A hilarious collection of preposterous, genuine email exchanges between comedy genius Bob and his victims'
Source

'Bob is a serious man, a thoughtful man, a complicated man, who knows that when holding a man's cock in the bathroom you look straight ahead. In the days where we can't open our e-mail inbox without being bombarded with stories of woe that only a large cash advance can solve, it's nice to know Bob's telling our stories too'
Sharp Magazine

'Some of the funniest e-mails you will ever read [and] some of the best comedy I have read in a while. If you ever wanted to "get even" with spammers, live vicariously through Bob Servant. The ride is wild and extremely funny'
Lunch.com

'This book will most certainly entertain and amuse. If getting "a live one" is akin to fly-fishing, these guys are the stars of the Fishing Channel and hilariously show internet-scam artists are just as gullible as their victims, if not more so. *Delete This At Your Own Peril* is funnier than 365 joke-of-the-day emails as the spammers realise they are dealing with a raving loony'
Serious Comedy Site

'After I finished being sick with laughter, I finally get round to writing a review. You can do the old fella a favour by purchasing his excellent book or just send him the money because he'll only go back to window cleaning to fund his jazz mag collection'
www.scaryduck.blogspot.com

'These are the writings of a clearly deranged mind'
Soteria

Delete This At Your Peril

Also by Bob Servant

Bob Servant – Hero of Dundee

Also by Neil Forsyth

Non Fiction

Other People's Money – The Rise and Fall of Britain's Most Audacious Fraudster (with Elliot Castro)

Fiction

Let Them Come Through

Delete This At Your Peril

The Bob Servant Emails

Bob Servant

with Neil Forsyth

BIRLINN

This edition published in 2010 by
Birlinn Limited
West Newington House
10 Newington Road
Edinburgh
EH9 1QS

www.birlinn.co.uk

First published in 2007 by Aurum Press Ltd, London

2

ISBN: 978 1 84158 919 0

British Library Cataloguing-in-Publication Data
A catalogue record for this book is available from the British Library

Designed and typeset by Brinnoven, Livingston
Printed and bound by CPI Cox & Wyman, Reading, RG1 8EX

Contents

For my big brother Alan, with love

Introduction:
Meet Bob Servant

I remember the first time I saw Bob Servant very well. It was in the late 1980s and I was a ten-year-old cycling through Broughty Ferry when I saw a burger van opening for business down at the harbour. This was a novel event both for me and, it would turn out, for Broughty Ferry and I skilfully reined in my Raleigh Burner and watched the momentous scene unfold. There were a couple of glum-looking men sprucing the van up, switching on ovens and so on, but my attention was drawn to another man who sat on a nearby bench watching them and occasionally offering words of advice that appeared to go largely unheeded.

I can really remember only a few details. One is that Bob had a bright red face, another is that he was drinking what I thought at the time was a milkshake but I now strongly suspect was a cocktail, and the final thing I can remember was what he said. He said, with an epic sense of despair, 'Fuck me Frank, watch the fucking sausages.'

The next time I saw Bob was perhaps five years later when I opened my bedroom curtains and there he was at the other side. The suddenness of my appearance caught him unawares and for a moment Bob threatened to fall off his ladder but he caught himself and gripped the window frame, panting and sweating and saying, 'Christ, you nearly fucking did for me there son.'

Bob, it seemed, had taken over the window-cleaning round that included our house. I can recall my mum's confusion at the increased frequency of the window-cleaning team's appearance. 'Someone's making a bloody fortune,' my dad used to summarise when he returned from work to hear of yet another visit.

Bob and I quickly became not friends, but certainly firm associates. For a bored schoolboy, Bob was a man of the world who advised with little encouragement on anything from women to feverish speculation on local thefts, and his ongoing feud with a local newspaper. For Bob, I was a willing listener, and the search for willing listeners has probably been the great cause of Bob's life.

In the winter Bob would appear on Saturday mornings, scaling his ladder dressed for Kilimanjaro rather than our two-storey home. I would crack open the frosted glass and it would begin. Both he and I would be going independently to watch Dundee United in the afternoon and, from deep within his array of padding, Bob would offer a range of optimistic predictions as steam rose from his bucket and multiple layers.

In the summer, Bob would curl a thick arm over the windowsill and start, usually with:

'Ah, how you doing? I was just saying to Frank there . . .'

And then he would unleash a story, a joke or, often, a plan. Bob's plans were extraordinary, containing an audacious mixture of ambition and completely undiluted self-belief. He toyed for a long time with entering local politics for what he called a clean-up campaign. That plan was quietly abandoned when Bob and Frank, whom he had appointed his election agent, could not decide on a suitable slogan.

Frank, I should point out, was Bob's regular window-cleaning sidekick and, I presumed (correctly), the original Frank from the burger van. Sometimes there would be other men with Bob, all of whose grave moods would clash markedly with his, but Frank was the standard. Perhaps because of this sustained exposure to Bob's peculiarities, Frank's depressive air was almost overpowering.

While Bob was halfway into my bedroom explaining how he was going to build a private zoo, or complete the Dawson Park monkey bars course in less than a minute, or swim the River Tay once things warmed up a bit, I would peek down to Frank, who would be standing at the foot of Bob's ladder.

At the very best he would look crushingly bored. At worst I would sometimes catch him staring at Bob's ladder with a distant look in his eyes, as if calculating just how many of life's worries would vanish with a hefty kick.

It was a few years on, when my friends and I began sneaking into Broughty Ferry's bars, that I saw a different side to Bob. His window-cleaning operation had been passed to strangers but his message on the matter was very clear.

'Not to worry,' he told me with an elaborate wink, along with the much-repeated suggestion that he had landed a significant windfall on the round to go with the riches from his years as the owner of a cheeseburger van.

There was also something about gypsies stealing his ladders that always sounded to me like a botched insurance job. Once, emboldened by drink, I put forward that theory to Bob, who replied with a quote from Winston Churchill that bore no relation to the situation whatsoever.

It became strange to walk into a Broughty Ferry pub and for Bob not to be there. If the place were quiet he would be hunched over a barstool, lecturing the barman and jabbing a finger to make his point. In busier pubs he would retreat with companions to a table, though this didn't stop the barman being generously incorporated by Bob into his conversation.

He had an eclectic collection of associates who you will soon discover are in his thoughts to this day. There was a uniformed security guard, a local lawyer who had been struck off and a group of traffic wardens who I'm sure were supposed to be working at the time. But more often than not, Bob's immediate company would be drawn from any combination of three men.

There was a small, sharp-faced man known as Tommy Peanuts who wore a suit with loosened tie, which did not seem to halt daytime excursions through the pubs of Broughty Ferry. He was quick with the cutting remark and often this would be aimed at an unknowing Bob's expense. I would feel a strange pang of shared betrayal when Tommy slipped in some mockery and Bob laughed innocently away.

Chappy Williams and Bob were locked in a love–hate relationship that clearly still rumbles along. The two should be brothers, such is the inherent rivalry as they compete for social standing in the bars of Broughty Ferry. This battle is generally waged through incredibly intricate practical jokes often taking days, if not weeks, in planning and execution.

And then there was, and is, Frank. A man referred to by Bob with, I believe, genuine fondness as Frank the Plank. As I gained increased access to Frank's company I realised very quickly that he wavers spectacularly on the very edge of sanity. Much of this is undoubtedly due to living next door to Bob. Whatever warped scheme or activity Bob is indulging in, you never have to look far to find Frank.

So that, for me, was Bob Servant. I moved away from Dundee, and a highlight of any return would be a chance meeting with Bob, for whom nothing ever really changed except the steady flow of ideas. He thought for a long time about opening a café, only to give up in fury when someone else did the same. He started another clean-up campaign which started and finished with him shopping a corrupt member of the local Limbo Walking Club to local press. He declared to myself and other astonished drinkers that he was going to buy a pair of ostriches and mate them in his garden (he never did).

But away from thwarted dreams, Bob had been doing something else. It was something that no one knew about and it was when I became the first person to be told that the relationship between Bob and myself changed forever.

* * *

As I sat reading a newspaper in a Broughty Ferry bar of an evening in early 2007, a familiar combination of reddened forehead and bunnet appeared above the page. It was Bob and he wanted to talk, but there was something different about him. There was none of his usual grandstanding and he employed a nervous whisper, darting his eyes around the pub in fear.

He confirmed that I was a writer and then slipped into a muddled explanation of some strange pursuit he had undertaken after winning a computer in a raffle at the local bowling club. He talked of Africans and

Russians, of emails and computers, and hinted at long nights of cheap wine and Internet exchanges.

'I mean,' he said with a sly grin, 'They're chancers, these people, Neil, real cowboys, but we've had some fun.'

Intrigued, I accepted Bob's invitation to learn more. We walked through the darkened streets in near silence, with Bob occasionally attempting further description only to give up in frustration or an extended bout of laughter. To be perfectly honest, I was a little nervous. Bob's eccentricity was all very well in public but, on the way to his house with him babbling about lions and rubber belts, it was slightly disturbing.

My alarm increased when we arrived at Bob's home. Although an impressive sight from outside, the interior was a study in chaos. There were collections of empty bottles throughout, various pieces of fancy dress hung from doorframes and an extraordinary number of novelty duvet sets. After we weaved through to the living room Bob directed me to a computer that he activated and went to get us drinks.

As the computer warmed up I noticed some scraps of paper beside the keyboard with scribbled notes. Amongst the jottings were names with arrows connecting to startling terms. 'Lanzhou', for example, pointed to 'rubber belts', which in turn pointed to 'stuff Clive's mouth with prawn crackers'. Bob returned with the drinks and brought up an email account on the screen.

'That's it,' he said simply and retired to a couch on which he lay in silent contemplation as I made my first entry into a very different world. An hour or two later I turned back to him.

'Bob?' I asked, 'Would you be interested in writing a book?'

Neil Forsyth and Bob Servant (right), Broughty Ferry, summer 2007

Each man is a hero and an oracle to somebody, and to that person whatever he says has an enhanced value.

Ralph Waldo Emerson (1803–82)

The thing is Xiong, you're over there in China and I'm here in Broughty Ferry. But you're just a man and I'm just a man. That's what I'm saying. We're all just men. Apart from women.

Bob Servant (1945–)

1
Lions, Gold and Confusion

From: Jack Thompson
To: Bob Servant
Subject: Delete This At Your Peril

FROM HIS ROYAL HIGHNEST, JACK THOMPSON

Dear sir,
Permit me to inform you of my desire of going into business. I got your name and contact from the chamber of commerce and industry. I am JACK THOMPSON, the only son of late King Arawi of tribal land. My father was a very wealthy traditional ruler, poisoned to death by his rivals in the traditional tussle about royalties and related matters.

Before his death here in Togo he called me on his sick bed and told me of a trunk box containing $75m kept in a security company where i amin the city of Sokode. It was because of the wealth he was poisoned by his rivals. I now seek a foreign partner where I will transfer the proceeds for investment as you may advise. I am willing to offer you 20% of the sum as a compensation for your effort/ input and 5% for any expenses that may occour.

Anticipating to hear from you soon.

Thanks and God bless

JACK THOMPSON

From: Bob Servant
To: Jack Thompson
Subject: Greetings

Good morning your Majesty,
I want 30%, and not a penny less,

Your Servant,

Bob Servant

From: Jack Thompson
To: Bob Servant
Subject: I will speak to the bank

Hello Bob,
See these percentages was arranged by the bank and not me. If you insist on getting 30% of the money i have to call the bank.

Pls send your

FULL NAME.
CONTACT PHONE NUMBER.
ACCOUNT NUMBER.
COUNTRY/STATE:

I will be expecting those details.thanks.

JACK THOMPSON.

From: Bob Servant
To: Jack Thompson
Subject: Good luck with the bank

Your Majesty,
Let me know what the bank says. Tomorrow's a bank holiday here, I
don't know if you have the same ones? My full name is BOB GODZILLA
SERVANT.

Yours,

Bob

From: Jack Thompson
To: Bob Servant
Subject: Hello

Hello Bob,
I went to my bank. If you are now requesting 30% we have to go back
to the high court to change things. I and my family members has added
some amount upon your money provided you are going to be serious and
trustwordy. We have agreed to give you 25%. Pls i think that is all we can
do.
    We need your telephone number, country, state, city and account
number before we can go further.

Jack Thompson

From: Bob Servant
To: Jack Thompson
Subject: Let's try the court

Good Morning Your Highness,
Please go to the High Court and request the 30%, I think it is a fair figure
Jacky-O.

Bob

From: Jack Thompson
To: Bob Servant
Subject: YOUR URGENT RESPONSE NEEDED

Dear Mr Bob,
In order not to waste more time I have agreed the 30% and have notified
the court and my family accordingly. Within these few days now, I
have developed that confidence in you and believe that you will be of
great assistance in perfecting this transaction. We have to go ahead
immediately. Please email me –

1. Your address
2. Private Telephone and Fax Numbers
3. Banking details to enable transfer of the money to you.

I await your immediate response,

Jack Thompson

From: Bob Servant
To: Jack Thompson
Subject: Hold Tight...

Your Highness,
I have been looking at the sums again, and I have decided that I want
40%.

And not a penny less.

Bob

From: Jack Thompson
To: Bob Servant
Subject: URGENT FROM MR JACK THOMPSON

Dear Bob,
Please let us PROCEDE. I am not greedy. I will offer you the 40%
instead of delaying the transaction. I want it done, no matter how little it
will change my life. Send your details now. Like I told you I need to meet
with the security company immediately,
    I await an urgent response,

Jack

From: Bob Servant
To: Jack Thompson
Subject: Taxman

Jack,

40% sounds about right. However, I do not want the money in cash, as there is no way I could hide it. The taxman tried to turn me over back in '89 when I was coining it in from the cheeseburger vans, and those bastards always come back.

Can I have my share in diamonds and gold? I can shift it gradually through pawnshops in Lochee.

Bob

From: Jack Thompson
To: Bob Servant
Subject: URGENT

Hello Bob,

I received your mail and I guess I understand it. As for the diamond and gold, I think I have access to raw gold. You will get your share in some amount of cash and some valuable quantity of gold. Look Bob you are wasting some time in forwarding your details that I need urgently. So now that we have come to an agreement can I have the details now please,

Thanks,

Jack

From: Bob Servant
To: Jack Thompson
Subject: Animals?

Hello Jack,

I'm afraid I just cannot take my share in cash, too dangerous. I could take it in diamonds, gold, or livestock (lions). My neighbour, Frank Theplank, has a private zoo. I just caught up with him in Maciocia's chip shop where he was waiting on a bag of fifty fritters for his monkeys. I told him a little bit about all this and he is willing to pay $80,000 for every lion I can get him,

Bob

From: Jack Thompson
To: Bob Servant
Subject: URGENT

Hello Bob,
I understand what you mean. You don't want the money in cash. Well I just got in contact with a friend of mine who sells raw gold and I can now pay you through live stock lion heads raw gold…quantity (4). So now you need not worry about the taxman coming again you can always keep them in your friend's private zoo as you said.

Now I will go and arrange for them while you send me your full details of yourself.

Jack

From: Bob Servant
To: Jack Thompson
Subject: Lions

Hi Jack my friend,
Great to hear from you again. You can get hold of 4 lions? Are they male or female? I will speak to Frank who will undoubtedly be very excited. Where are these lions just now?

Bob

From: Jack Thompson
To: Bob Servant
Subject: URGENT DETAILS PLEASE

Hello Bob,
The gold lions are all male and i have arranged for them. But Bob can't you see you are dragging us backwards i have been asking you for your details for the past days now. Pls reply with the following:

Full Name
Home Address
Phone/Fax Number
Banking Details

I will be expecting the above information.

Thanks.

Jack

From: Bob Servant
To: Jack Thompson
Subject: OK

Jack my friend,
OK, things are now progressing. My full name is, as you know, Bob
Godzilla Servant
68 Harbour View Road,
Broughty Ferry,
Dundee[1]

It's a lovely spot Broughty Ferry, and I stay down near the river. There's not
much traffic which is obviously perfect, as otherwise the lions would get
rattled. Can you please send me a photo of the lions without delay? I need
to see that you definitely have access to them, before I confirm things with
that halfwit Frank.

Your friend,

Bob

From: Jack Thompson
To: Bob Servant
Subject: Details

Hello Bob,
Hope fine. The informations you gave me not complete, you only gave me
your full name and your address. I will need–

Country
State
City
Zip Code
Phone Number
Bank Account

Pls give me the above information then we can proceed. As for the lions,
I have to take some photographs of them before I scan and send to you,
so you have to give me some time. Pls provide me with the remaining
information Bob.

Thanks,

Jack

---

1. Bob does indeed live near the River Tay, and in some style, but this address
does not exist. Just in case anyone was thinking of visiting.

From: Bob Servant
To: Jack Thompson
Subject: Here you go champ

Jack my friend,
What a wonderful morning, hope it's a belter over there in Togo also.

Zip Code - ▄▄▄▄▄▄
City - Dundee
Country - Scotland

I'll get the information from the bank later on. The Bank of Scotland in Broughty Ferry closes early on a Wednesday so the staff can go tenpin bowling.[2] Please get the photos of the lions to me as soon as you can, then we can move on. I cannot wait to see those magnificent creatures. Are they currently in captivity, or will you actually be capturing them yourself? By Christ Jack, I wish I were on that hunt with you my friend. Helping you. And holding you.

Yours Faithfully,

Bob G Servant

From: Jack Thompson
To: Bob Servant
Subject:
Pictures of the raw lions

Hello Bob,
You didn't include phone number or bank account. I have made arrangement in transporting the 4 gold lions to you. I have put photos below. One costs $299,000 so 4 will cost over $1,196,000 then the rest will be in cash. These gold lions will be bought from a friend of mine's company. So give me your phone number for better communication and bank information,

Thanks,

Jack

---

2. The Bank of Scotland in Broughty Ferry does not close early on a Wednesday so the staff can go tenpin bowling.

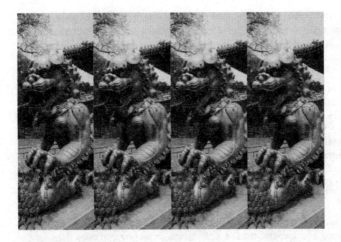

From: Bob Servant
To: Jack Thompson
Subject: You have got to be kidding?

Jack,

Sorry about the delay, I was out getting my hair done. There appears to have been a slight misunderstanding my friend, I was expecting four live lions, not gold ones. If I stuck four lion statues in Frank's zoo then he would think I'd lost the fucking plot and would tell everyone that I'd gone mental again like when I first got the cheeseburger van money through and wore that dinosaur poncho for four months. The four photos you sent look great, if a little similar, but I'm afraid that you seem to have got the wrong end of the stick.

Bob

From: Jack Thompson
To: Bob Servant
Subject: URGENT

Hello Bob,

Hope fine. Sorry I misunderstood you, 4 live lions will be much easier for me.

Look Bob, I went to that security company yesterday i was told to get $4000 to process the document for retrieval of the boxes that contains the money. I have raised $2000 so i need you to assist me in the rest of the money. Immediately you send the remaining $2000 I will go to the security company so they can release the funds and I will purchase the lions immediately. I will pay you back the money with percentages.

This is urgent, reply immediately.

Jack

From: Bob Servant
To: Jack Thompson
Subject: No Problem

Jack,
OK, can you send me the photos of the live lions? Where are you getting them? I will speak to the bank tomorrow, but $2,000 sounds fine, how much is that in pounds? The exchange rates in the Dundee *Evening Telegraph* are bollocks, they're done by the same guy that does the horoscopes.[3]

Bob

From: Jack Thompson
To: Bob Servant
Subject: HURRY BOB

Hello Bob,
Bob $2000 is £1700. Pls try to send it so I can collect the fund from the security company and as well send the lions to you. These is the lion's picture below. I have made arrangement of transporting it to you. I am buying four male lions from my friends private zoo and he has also arranged for shipment to Scotland.

I will prefer you send the money through Western Union transfer, so I can collect the fund and start shipping the lions.

Thanks,

Jack

---

3. This is entirely untrue. Dundee's *Evening Telegraph* newspaper carries a precise reflection of the day's exchange rates.

From: Bob Servant
To: Jack Thompson
Subject: LION PICTURE

Jack,
Greetings my dear, dear friend. Jacky, there seems to have been another misunderstanding. I looked at the website that is listed on the photo of the lion you sent and it belongs a Boston-based author and nature lover.

"I'm Tony Northrup. I live with my wife and cat in Woburn, Massachusetts, which is about 8 miles North-West of Boston", he states quite clearly on his site.

Now Jack, I'm not sure if I can see the connection between yourself and Tony. Perhaps you sent the wrong photo?

Bob

From: Jack Thompson
To: Bob Servant
Subject: YOU MISUNDERSTAND

Hello Bob,
You are getting this all wrong Bob. I didn't say that was the exact lion, I only gave you a clue on how the lion I will send looks like. If you want to see the exact lion I will send you must give me time to take it and scan it.

So Bob my friend you don't need to worry over this. This is Africa and you well know these animals are sufficient here. My brother even rears a cub that's a baby lioness in his house, so Bob expect the lion's photograph later today. You haven't said anything about the money I asked for? Have you spoken to your bank? I don't think £1,700 should take long to send?

Thanks,

Jack

From: Bob Servant
To: Jack Thompson
Subject: OK, I get it.

Hi Jack,
Thanks so much for putting my mind at rest and letting me know what a lion looks like. I have seen them in the past, in books and suchlike, so already had a fair idea but you have really helped me out there. For example, I had it in my head for some stupid reason that lions wore spectacles.

I look forward to seeing the photo of the actual lions. I just popped my head over the garden wall and had a word with Frank. He was busy cleaning out his Flamingo cage but he did say that he is very, very excited about getting hold of these lions. He has asked me to pass on a few questions –

Are they male or female?
Are they in good physical condition?
Do they talk?

Thank you my friend, and don't worry, I have booked in to see the bank manager tomorrow morning,

Bob

From: Jack Thompson
To: Bob Servant
Subject: URGENT

Hello Bob,
Hope fine.

Answer to the questions.

1. The lions are all male lions and are very healthy.

2. I don't think I have ever seen a lion that talks.

I don't know if you are also interested in leopards cause my friend works in the Government Zoo and he could find a leopard for you? Remember to speak to your bank tomorrow.

Thanks,

Jack

From: Bob Servant
To: Jack Thompson
Subject: Leopards

I have spoken to Frank. He will take two leopards as long as they are friendly, and one elephant if you can get it? Frank is sure that he saw a talking lion on the television once. He thinks it was either on Songs of Praise or Bullseye. He says it reminded him of Jim McLean, the old Dundee United manager. Are you sure you can't get one?

I am going to the bank in two hours,

Bob

From: Jack Thompson
To: Bob Servant
Subject: URGENT

Hello Bob,
Hope fine. I can get you two leopards. They are both not adults. I will try and see if the elephant will be possible and will see what I can do for the lion. When you are back from bank mail me and tell me when you are sending the money.

Thanks,

Jack.

From: Bob Servant
To: Jack Thompson
Subject: The Full List

Jack,
How are you my friend? Frank just called, he will take the following –

4 lions, 2 leopards, 1 elephant, 1 alligator, 2 parrots, 1 hedgehog.

I said you might be able to get the two leopards and the elephant. How are you looking for the rest? And, of course, the talking lion? Frank has a good few quid. He's worked for me on various bits and bobs and I've always looked after him so I think we should put our necks out on this one and make sure the lions talk.

Bob

From: Jack Thompson
To: Bob Servant
Subject: URGENT

Hello Bob.
From your mail I will only be able to get

4 lions
2 leopards
1 Alligator

The hedgehog, parrots and elephant will take me some time to find but I think I will first send the four lions and two leopards to you before we proceed with the rest. Bob please send the £1,700 now so I can send the 4 lions and 2 leopards to you. I think one of the lions may talk a little.

Thanks,

Jack.

From: Bob Servant
To: Jack Thompson
Subject: Sounds good

Hi Jack, I will pass on the bad news to Frank on the hedgehog front. I'm not sure about a lion that only talks a little, I'd like one that isn't so shy if possible?

Bob

From: Jack Thompson
To: Bob Servant
Subject: THIS IS URGENT

Bob: This is urgent. What is hapening?? I don't sell animals. I only said I could get some lions to help you. Then you say you need a leopard and I say ok. Now you are saying the lion has to talk? What is this madness? Send me the £1700 that we agreed imeediately.

Jack

From: Bob Servant
To: Jack Thompson
Subject: Take it easy Jack

Jack,
What does the lion say when it talks? I am just checking that it won't get
me into any fights.

Your servant,

Bob Servant

From: Jack Thompson
To: Bob Servant
Subject: THIS IS URGENT

BOB LETS GO STRAIGHT TO THE POINT. THE LIONS AND
LEOPARDS ARE HERE WITH ME AT THE BACK OF MY HOUSE
THEY ARE FRIENDLY AND ONE OF THE LION TALKS. BOB
SEND ME THE £1700 SO I CAN COLLECT THAT MONEY AND
SHIP THEM TO YOU.

JACK

From: Bob Servant
To: Jack Thompson
Subject: Take it easy Jack

Jack,
Things are coming along nicely. I just need to know, for Frank's
benefit more than anything –

What are the names of the lions? (he needs to know what to call
them when they are introduced)

What does the lion say when it talks? (Again, who wants a lion that'll
get them into scraps?)

The bank is preparing me some forms,

Bob

From: Jack Thompson
To: Bob Servant
Subject: HERE IS THE INFORMATION

Hello Bob,

We have really wasted much time. Anyway, the information you asked for

1. The lion with more hair is Captain

2. The lion with black hair is Zoro

The other two do not have names, you can give them names yourself. And as for the lion that talks it's ways of talking are strange. It does not pronounce words well it only makes sounds. Hope you understand now. Bob the security company has given me a day's grace. This is very serious, I don't think you realise what we are about to lose. Let me know when you will send the money and I will give you the info for Western Union.

Jack

From: Bob Servant
To: Jack Thompson
Subject: All looking good...

Hello Jack,
Sorry about the delay. I was round at Frank's earlier and got stuck up a tree whilst chasing a snake, then fell off and banged my head on a chicken. You know what it's like. Listen Jack, the bank needs to know which account and country the money would be going to? I had extended discussions with Frank at Doc Ferry's bar this evening and he is absolutely delighted with the way things are going. He wants to know a last couple of things –

Can he call the other lions 'FANCY PANTS', and 'BRYAN'? Do the leopards sing, and are they willing to wear clothes?

All the best babes,

Bob

From: Jack Thompson
To: Bob Servant
Subject: GO TO WESTERN UNION

Hello Bob,
Sorry for what happened to you, hope you didn't get injured. Tell your bank to send the money through Western Union. Money transfer to:

Name: ██████
Country: ██████

State/City: ███████
Branch: ████████

This is my very good friend name and address that is working in the bank. You will have to set a secret Question and Answer and be sure to send me the answer.

As for the lions you can call them any name provided you shout when talking to them and always use the same name. And trained leopards like the one I have for you will wear any clothes you buy for them OK. Please send the money today,

Jack

From: Bob Servant
To: Jack Thompson
Subject: Nearly back to 100%

Hello my good friend,
Thanks so much for your kind words. I have nearly fully recovered from the fall and have just been chilling out ever since. I've still got a large bandage on my head however, and am too embarrassed to leave the house as then I'd have to tell people how I got the injury. The boys would love this one. If Tommy Peanuts or Chappy Williams got hold of it I'd not be able to show my face for weeks.

I should be OK tomorrow and will nip up to the bank then. Just a quick question about the leopard, does it look a bit like this?

Good luck my friend,

Bob

From: Jack Thompson
To: Bob Servant
Subject: URGENT

HELLO BOB,
I HOPE YOU ARE GETTING BETTER. I RECEIVED YOUR MAIL,
SINCE YOU SAID TODAY YOU WILL BE GOING TO THE BANK
PLEASE GO THERE RIGHT AWAY. AS FOR THE LEOPARD
THE SKIN ARE ALIKE, THAT'S THE WAY IT LOOKS LIKE, SO
PLEASE TRY AS MUCH AS YOU CAN TO RECOVER SO YOU CAN
BE ABLE TO GO TO THE BANK. I WILL BE EXPECTING YOUR
REPLY SOONEST.

THANKS.

JACK

From: Bob Servant
To: Jack Thompson
Subject: What a Let Down

Jack,
I have some bad news my friend. I have just been to the bank and the
guy there said that I cannot send you any money as I do not have any in
my account. In actual fact, it turns out that I owe them over eight grand. I
tried to explain that I needed to send you this money for the lions and the
leopard but the guy said I was a fucking lunatic and got the security man to
throw me out.

   I'm really sorry Jack, I hope I haven't wasted your time in any way, I
can't see how I could have, but I'm afraid that the deal is off. Good luck
my friend, and good luck with the animals. If they get too much then you'd
probably be OK just releasing them?

Love,

Bob

From: Jack Thompson
To: Bob Servant
Subject: Urgent

Hello Bob,
You see do you really still need lions and leopard? I will help you out
sending it for you free but what you only have to do is to send just $700 or
$500 for shipping it to Scotland.

If you can go to another bank to send that money to me just take the money from home and tell them you want to send that money through Western Union money transfer to that name i gave to you earlier on. It is easy. Do it today.

Jack

From: Jack Thompson
To: Bob Servant
Subject: Urgent

Bob?

No Reply

2
Bob and the Postie

From: Jean Kitson
To: Bob Servant
Subject: Employment Format

Sir,

Polysmooth is a UK textile company. We produce and distribute clothing materials worldwide and are looking for people to assist us with a new distribution network.

MAIN REQUIREMENTS

18 years or older, legally capable, responsible, to work 3-4 hours per week, with PC knowledge, e-mail and internet experience (minimal).

And please know that Everything is absolutely legal, that's why You have to fill a contract! If you are interested, please respond with your details. Thanks for your anticipated action.

Very Respectfully,

Mr. President,
Polysmooth International

ENGLAND

Best Regards

Jean Kitson

From: Bob Servant
To: Jean Kitson
Subject: Re: Employment Format

I might be interested Jean. But right now I have some legal problems to take care of.

Your Servant,

Bob Servant

From: Jean Kitson
To: Bob Servant
Subject: Re: Employment Format

Hope the problem is not that serious but you can share with me if you think I have to know about it.

From: Bob Servant
To: Jean Kitson
Subject: Re: Employment Format

I am in big trouble. Do you know any lawyers?

I have money.

From: Jean Kitson
To: Bob Servant
Subject: Re: Employment Format

Sure, i know some i can introduce you to my lawyer, he is here in the UK, what do you really want? If he can assist you then i'll tell him, hope to hear from you soon

Jean Kitson

From: Bob Servant
To: Jean Kitson
Subject: My shame

Jean,
Great, can you please forward this to the lawyer –

DO NOT JUDGE ME BECAUSE I AM A GOOD MAN.

My name is Bob Servant. You might well have heard of me from the days when I ran the Ellieslea Road to Beach Avenue windowcleaning round. It was Howard Reoch's beat for years but Howie lost it with the OVD and ended up shacking up with a Chinese girl in Lochee and only leaving the flat to get his hair cut.

Anyway, I had to sell the round ten years ago when some little fucker stole my ladders.[4] From there things just turned really bad. I stopped getting work other than from bungalows, and it just wasn't enough to run the van on. So then I was down to bungalows that I could reach on foot and there are only really four of them. It got to the stage I was turning up at those four houses a couple of times a week, then nearly every day and they soon rumbled that I was taking the piss and sacked me. So that was me.

---

4. The story behind the loss of Bob's ladders in 1996 remains unclear. If forced, I would conclude that they were not stolen, but sold as part of the deal through which Bob disposed of his window-cleaning business. However, that should not be seen as evidence in the evaluation of any insurance claim made by Bob at the time.

Since then I spend my time as a 'man about town'. Sometimes this is a great life, but other times I get quite low. I sit in my house, eating jaffa cakes, drinking cheap wine and building duvet dens in the front room. It's no kind of life, no kind of life at all.

Anyway, I found a way of livening things up, which was to play pranks on my postman. His name is Trevor and he is a complete prick. At first it was basic stuff - I'd grab the letters out his hand and pretend to be a dog, or sit up on the roof and chuck a bucket of water over him.

He complained to the police and they warned me off but that just annoyed me because what did he have to go and tell them for? So I really went to town on him. I built a hide in the garden and took pot-shots at him with an air rifle or chucked a firework at his head. It was really funny. You should have seen his face the time I hit him square on the napper with the Catherine Wheel. I think he might have been crying.

Things came to a head last week. I hid behind a tree and jumped out with a hose but he saw me in time and rushed me. He got his sack over my head but I fought back and managed to get him on the ground. At this point the weasel managed to squirm away but I grabbed him round the top of his trousers and at the same time went for him with the hose.

Unfortunately, he pulled away again and both his trousers and pants came off in my left hand whilst, with my right hand, I accidentally shoved the hosepipe up his bottom. The first I knew was when he let out the most incredible scream, I've never heard anything like it. I threw off the sack and realised what had happened but by that time he was hopping down the path, howling away with the top of the hose still protruding out of his arse. He looked a bit like the Australian kangaroo.

Anyway, to cut a long story short these are the charges that I face as a result of that moment of madness –

ASSAULT
SEXUAL ASSAULT
HARRASSMENT
EXTREME EMBARRASSMENT

I am in court in two weeks – Can you help? What's the best defence? I hope we can work together on this,

Thank you,
Bob

From: Jean Kitson
To: Bob Servant
Subject: Re: My shame

I can help you if you want to help yourself, i was going to give you 7% of the check money we are sending to you, but because of the problem you have I talked to the rest of the company board and they said we would offer you $1000 not $700 and if in the long run you did your job well, you might get rewarded more. What you have to do now is get back to me with all your personal and banking details so we can register you as a worker.

Best regards

Jean Kitson

From: Bob Servant
To: Jean Kitson
Subject: Eh?

Jean,
Thank you for your help but that is no good. I do not need a job, what I need is a lawyer and I need one urgently. I'd use Pop Wood but the guy's legal qualifications are only currently recognised in various Broughty Ferry bars.

Good luck for the future,

Thanks,

Bob

From: Jean Kitson
To: Bob Servant
Subject: I already contacted my attorney

No Bob,
I already contacted my attorney just didn't tell you what he said because I thought you wanted a job. He is willing to come help you at the court so you can be free without charges but he will need you to send him his ticket fee and also pay up front some of the amount to be paid in total after the case is done. Are you also here in the UK, or in another country? Let me know so i can tell the attorney.

Best Regards

Jean Kitson

From: Bob Servant
To: Jean Kitson
Subject: OK

Yes, I am in the UK, up in Scotland. Can you please tell me what the attorney's idea is for my defence? Personally, I think it is very important that I had the sack over my head at the time of the so-called sexual assault. I could not see so how could I have known where the hose was going to go? X-ray specs?

Bob

From: Jean Kitson
To: Bob Servant
Subject: He said he will fill a document

Bob,
OK he said he will fill a document that shows you were not feeling good then and that you didn't do it intentionally, he said that will work. The travelling fee to Scotland isnt much, about £950 plus the upfront money of the case which is all together about £3000. Hope to hear from you soon so I know what to tell the Attorney. Stay safe,

Jean Kitson

From: Bob Servant
To: Jean Kitson
Subject: Chopper?

Jean,
£950 to get to Scotland? Is he coming by fucking helicopter? I think it would be best if you put me in touch with him directly please,

Thank you for your help,

Bob

From: Jean Kitson
To: Bob Servant
Subject: His email

His email is ▆▆▆▆▆▆▆▆▆▆▆▆▆▆▆ and his name is Tim Sanderson. Email him directly,

Regards

Jean Kitson

From: Bob Servant
To: Tim Sanderson
Subject: Hello there

Howdy,
I believe that Jean Kitson has explained my case to you, I am looking for
a lawyer to come and defend me on some trumped up charges. If you are
interested in my case, then please tell me what you think the best defence
would be. If it sounds strong enough, I will retain you immediately,

All the best,

Bob Servant

From: Tim Sanderson
To: Bob Servant
Subject: Hello there

Hello Mr Servant,
Yes my client Jean has explained things. It would be best for me to come
there so we can put our heads together.You'll have to send fees, then when
I come we can talk about your problem. But to start with I'm a good
Lawyer with first Class Upper professional degree so I believe I can get
you out of this mess.

Just one good point I'll make now and the others you will wait till I
come and we can talk better. From the mail Jean passed to me, I'll say
you are at fault but suffered harassment for a long time. So, to get you
out of this mess, a suggestion is putting up a genuine lie backed up with
evidence which the court will accept. I'll tell the court you had a mental
disorder for more than a month (it will match the time you started this
trouble of yours) and will give them a letter from the psychiatrist hospital.

We therefore plead you didn't know what you were doing so all the
harassment, embarrassment, and sexual harassment could be put to an
end and the case could be stopped. Well, I think with just this point you
are probably already convinced that I am capable to get you out of this?

Hope to hear from you soon, so we could make arrangement on how
you are going to send me the money with your details and how to get to
you,

Best Regards,

Lawyer T. Sanderson

From: Bob Servant
To: Tim Sanderson
Subject: My defence

Tim,

I like your idea and I think it's just about crazy enough to work. However, I think I may have spotted a slight flaw. Where is the psychiatric hospital you'll get this letter from? It would maybe look a little strange for me to visit London to get my head examined?

By the way, that fucking postie is getting right on my tits again. He knows I can't touch him because of the court case so he's really rubbing my nose in it. When he delivers the mail he shouts stuff through the letterbox like, "Ooh, is this a letter from your boyfriend Bob?" and he sometimes scores out 'Bob' on the letters and writes 'Blob'. I just want to get him again but I have to stop myself because that will just get me in more trouble.

Bob

From: Tim Sanderson
To: Bob Servant
Subject: Just ignore him

Here is my number ███████████████ you can call me anytime. But Bob as for him getting on your nerves just ignore him. We will have to go to the nearest hospital to you, the one you are known better, that way it will be easy for us to get the letter.

Stay safe

Lawyer T. Sanderson

From: Bob Servant
To: Tim Sanderson
Subject: Flowers for Jean

Hello Tim,

You're right of course, but it's hard to ignore him sometimes. This morning I heard a tapping on the window and when I opened it he was standing outside urinating all over my front lawn. He was absolutely loving it, spraying everywhere and laughing at me. I don't know how much more I can take before I do something that I regret. I would love to call you but my phone has been cut off because of a Booty Express mix-up. I hope to have it working in the next few days.

I can't go to the hospital here Tim, I'm banned after a misunderstanding back in '94. Dundee United won the Scottish Cup and I read in the paper about how the players had taken the cup to see some sick kids at the hospital. I'd been drinking Snowballs in the Ferry Inn with a couple of traffic wardens (who were on duty at the time!) and so I stupidly decided that I would go and help cheer up the kids.

I made what I thought was an exact origami copy of the Scottish Cup but was really a mess of beer mats and sellotape and went and caught the bus. By the time I got there I was struggling to see but I remember the receptionist telling me that she didn't think my visit would be appropriate. She asked me for my address which I thought was for a Thank You letter but a week later I got a banning order.[5] Not to worry, we can attack them in other ways. Do you agree, for example, we should stress the fact that when the whole hose thing happened, the sack was still over my head? I think this is absolutely vital.

Also, I would really like to send Jean a small gift. She's a classy lady and I don't want to look cheap, but I don't want her to think I'm trying it on. I've got enough to worry about without getting myself a bird! Perhaps she'd like this fun tracksuit?

Bob

----

5. Bob Servant has never received a banning order from any of Dundee's hospitals. I do, however, remember seeing Bob on many occasions in the weeks after United's 1994 cup win struggling with an oversized, tin foil, imitation trophy.

From: Tim Sanderson
To: Bob Servant
Subject: Jean said you shouldn't bother

I talked to Jean she said you shouldn't bother, that I should say thank you and that she only did what she did because you needed help. When are you ready to send the money and when will I come?

Lawyer T. Sanderson

From: Bob Servant
To: Tim Sanderson
Subject: Good old Jean

Tim,

Typical Jean! What a wonderful woman. No, I want to send her a present, it's only fair, please give me her address and I'll send some flowers. Otherwise, I have access to a pedalo that she may be interested in? The Harbour Police use these to patrol Broughty Ferry harbour and watch out for Communists.[6] Jean will have to pay the postage however, which I estimate would be around £1,000.

Anyway, I need to go and set myself up for the postie's arrival, I have a special plan for him this morning,

Bob

From: Tim Sanderson
To: Bob Servant
Subject: Jean said you shouldn't bother

Nevermind about Jean Bob, she did not want anything. I've warned you to leave the postie and not hurt him just ignore him. Look Bob, I won't be having time to reply to more of your mail until you pay the fees. This is suffering my other clients. Message me when you want me to come with your address and airport name, and you can mail the money,

Stay safe

Lawyer T. Sanderson

---

6. Broughty Ferry does not have a Harbour Police service and, even if they did, it is unlikely they would use pedalos owing to weather and safety concerns.

From: Bob Servant
To: Tim Sanderson
Subject: I AM IN TROUBLE

Are you there?

Oh God what have I done?

From: Tim Sanderson
To: Bob Servant
Subject: Yes I am here

Yes Bob. How can I help?

From: Bob Servant
To: Tim Sanderson Subject:
Subject: It's got a little spicy

Tim,

It's the postie Tim, the fucking postie. I have him trapped in the cupboard under the stairs. Don't ask me how it happened, all I know is that I got drunk and when I woke up I was lying down in the kitchen. I heard a bit of moaning that I followed and found him. I have taken a photo for you.

What am I going to do? He says that if I let him go he will not tell anyone but how can I trust him? Would you be able to email me a legal

form that he could sign which would say that he couldn't go to the police and tell them?

I know you said £3,000 but if you can get me out of this new scrape I will pay you £5,000 because now I am really worried. If he goes to the police then I think I could be done for kidnapping.I have been looking after him, feeding him jaffa cakes and putting a little radio beside him and he says that he will tell people it was all a misunderstanding, that we were playing a game of sardines and it just got out of hand. But can I trust him?

Please help me Tim, and don't be angry, I know I've been a fool.

Bob

From: Tim Sanderson
To: Bob Servant
Subject: stay calm

I can help with this new situation but only if you pay half of my bills because it is now severe, thats my policy.

From: Bob Servant
To: Tim Sanderson
Subject: Absolutely no problem at all Timbo

Tim,
OK, will do. How much is half the bill? Things are going fine. I've untied Trevor apart from his legs and have been cooking nice meals for him. We had a great pasta dish earlier and I'm going to do a spaghetti Bolognese tonight. He says he's not that bothered about being tied up in the cupboard because it means he doesn't have to go to work and also that he doesn't really like his wife.

Bob

From: Tim Sanderson
To: Bob Servant
Subject: The half bill is

The half bill is £1500. You be careful and don't hurt him because if you do that's going to get you in a big trouble. You have done enough already, message me back with when you can wire the money and I'll send you my info. stay safe.

Tim

From: Bob Servant
To: Tim Sanderson
Subject: half bill

Hi Tim,

£1,500 is no problem. In Dundee's infamous Cheeseburger Wars of 1988–99, I had three vans working double shifts five days a week (I attach a photo of one of the vans in a cracking litle pitch, ready for another bumper day). Those vans were mobbed everywhere they went, it was unbelievable. It sounds funny thinking about it now, but no-one even knew what cheeseburgers were in Dundee before then.

People just went crazy for them.[7] I stuck the boys on £50 a shift and paid fuck-all tax. You do the math, Tim

You know, things are great here. I have been untying Trevor completely for one-hour stretches, which we call his 'Cry Freedoms', which makes us

7. A 1988 issue of the *Broughty Ferry Gazette* bore the headline, 'This Cheeseburger Madness Must Stop' and included claims from a local councillor that schoolchildren and 'those old enough to know better' were buying their breakfast, lunch and dinner from an 'Armada' of cheeseburger vans. The report quotes 'local cheeseburger magnate Bob Servant' as saying 'I'm giving the people what they want. The councillor will be telling us what time to go to bed next. He's just angry because I wouldn't give him an expenses slip with his burgers.'

both laugh. He can go to the toilet, have a stretch or just potter around the house for a while.

We're getting on well – we both love talking about women and eating jaffa cakes and earlier today he said I was his 'best friend'. I got all embarrassed and angry and tied him up again but, you know, I think he might have meant it. He's not a bad chap and I'm starting to think that maybe he won't tell the police,

Bob Servant

From: Tim Sanderson
To: Bob Servant
Subject: Safest way is Western Union

The best and safest way is through Western Union. What you will do is go to the nearest Western Union location to send the £1500. Here is my personal assistant details she will go get the money as soon as you send it cos i'm busy at the office.

Sarah Riley

██████████████

██████████████

BIRMINGHAM

████████

That's where she lives, she will go get the money. Email me with the necessary details so i can give it to her. Hope to hear from you soon.

Regards

Lawyer T. Sanderson

From: Bob Servant
To: Tim Sanderson
Subject: It's party time

Hi Tim,

Are you sure I shouldn't just post the cash? I could tape the money to a bit of card so it doesn't get nicked? Let me know because the £1,500 is ready to go. The postie and I are still going great guns but I think it's important to have a good legal defence just in case.

He's been untied for a couple of days but has not even mentioned going home. We just mess about, playing tig or designing putting courses. I make breakfast, he makes lunch and then the two of us do dinner together. It's a great system, and seems to be working fine.

The only slight problem we have is that I have always watched the evening showing of Neighbours but he is a massive Richard and Judy fan. So far he's settled for watching them until 5.35 and then we switch to Neighbours but I can see he's not happy with it. We have our tea at 5.30 and, yesterday, when I turned over to Neighbours he let some of his scrambled eggs drop onto the carpet and said 'Oh dear, I wonder if one of your Neighbours will help clean that up' in a really sarcastic voice. I did what you told me Tim, and just ignored him. But that's been the only moment that we've looked like falling out.

Tonight we're going to a fancy dress party that the postie's friend is having at his house. I can't wait, he says there's going to be loads of women there from the sorting office. Apparently, they're going to get blootered and then just go straight to work at five in the morning. They do it once a month apparently, the whole Dundee East Sorting Office, and the next day they just go and put letters in any postbox they fancy because they're still so drunk.[8] So God knows where my mail will end up tomorrow! Or in your case, Timorrow! Ha, ha. Silly.

I'm going to the party as a cowboy and the postie is going as a ghost. Are you going to a party tonight Tim? I bet you are, knowing you. What are you going as?

Bob

From: Tim Sanderson
To: Bob Servant
Subject: Western Union

Send the money to my assistant through Western Union as I said and email me the security details. Hope you are having a great party, i anticipate your response.

Regards

Lawyer T. Sanderson

From: Bob Servant
To: Tim Sanderson
Subject: Good News

Tim,
How are you my friend? Well, well, well, where to begin?! It has been the most mental two days of my life, which is pretty impressive considering I

---

8. The editor is of no doubt that Dundee East postal staff are of the highest professional integrity and I consider Bob's suggestion to be entirely delusional.

was officially mental for those four months in '89 when I was high on the hog with the cheeseburger van money.

Right, well let's start at the fancy dress party I told you about last time. We got to the door and the postie pressed the bell. Just as they opened the door he whipped his ghost sheet off and he was wearing his best gear - proper denim and a really nice V-neck. So there was him in his Saturday night turn, a couple of birds at the door looking confused, and me dressed as a fucking cowboy.

It wasn't a party at all, he'd arranged a double date with these goers from his work but thought it would be funny to make old muggins here turn up like Jesse fucking James. The worst bit was he didn't let them in on the joke, when they asked why I was wearing that stuff he told them that it was what I always wore when I went out.

I was so angry I couldn't even bring myself to say anything so I just walked through and we sat and had dinner with me still in the cowboy stuff. The postie was loving it. I tried to make some conversation but anything I said he'd give it 'yee-hah' or 'sorry we don't have any cow pie' which isn't even a cowboy joke, it was Desperate Dan that ate cow pie.

I was pretty annoyed and, I suppose, a little bit hurt and threw a bit of a tantrum. I shouted at the postie that he had let me down, that I had trusted him, and he'd made me look stupid. I went right off on one and I could see the girls were scared but I just kept going. At the end there was this horrible silence and then the postie started whistling the theme tune to Rawhide.

And you know what Tim? I laughed. That's right, I laughed. I laughed and I laughed and so did the postie and so did the girls and we just all started hugging each other. And then we were kissing and then one thing led to another Tim and, well, I won't say any more on that.

Tim, it was sensational. It's been a long time since I got properly involved with a bird and I have to say that I was worried old Bobby might not have much in the locker but by Christ I went to town on that bit of skirt. You should have seen me Tim, I was like a man possessed, I felt like a bloody kid up the back of the pictures.

Well, since then things have really gone very well indeed. The postie and I have decided that we are going to live together and spend our time chasing women like a couple of wild cards – throwing on the denim, downing some liveners, then heading into town and seeing what happens. Ach, we're probably just two old dreamers without half a brain between us Tim! But, my God, we'll give it a go.

So really it's all good news. The postie has promised me that he will drop the charges. Thanks for your help Tim and please thank Jean also. I know you'll both be happy for me, being the kind of people you are.

All the very best for the future,

Bob Servant

From: Tim Sanderson
To: Bob Servant
Subject: Western Union

I am glad things have gone well, please send £500 for the advice I gave you. Send it through Western Union to the details I provided.

From: Bob Servant
To: Tim Sanderson Subject:
Subject: Hands off the party fund!

Sorry, Tim. We have to watch our pennies as the postie has quit his job so he and I can chase skirt professionally. I'd be happy to act as a reference for any similar cases you find yourself involved with if that's any use?

Cheers,

Bob

No Reply

3
Alexandra, Bob and Champion

From: Alexandra
To: Bob Servant
Subject: Hello!

Hello, my new friend! My name is Alexandra, 25 years old. I live in Russia and want to get acquainted with man from other country. Be not surprised to my letter. I have learned your address in agency of international acquaintances. I do not know, like you my photo or not? At once I want to say I do not search the relation for games. I want to find the husband! I shall expect answer with impatience!

Best wishes, Alexandra

P.S. Please, send to me your photo.

From: Bob Servant
To: Alexandra
Subject: By Christ You Could Take Someone's Eyes Out With Them

Alexandra,
How are you? What a fantastic photo. My God, what a pair of bazookas. How is life over there in Russia?

Your Servant,

Bob Servant

From: Alexandra
To: Bob Servant
Subject: Hello!

Dear Bob!
I am very glad that you have answered my letter! It is a pity, that you have not sent me the photo. It is a problem for you? I live in city Vladivostok. Probably, you think me beautiful and think, that at me it is a lot of admirers. Yes, I shall not begin to deny it. But I do not like the Russian men, their attitude to women. I want to love and be loved. Unfortunately, I have not found it in the country. I am gentle women but I am a tiger when I am in love!

Alexandra

From: Bob Servant
To: Alexandra
Subject: YOU LIKE THE TIGER? I LIKE THE LION!

Alex,
A tiger eh? I can certainly sympathise with anyone who has a love of large cats, being an enormous lion fan. A lion is tough, it's bloody tough, but it doesn't bully people and has a great sense of humour.

A funny thing happened to me today in Woolworth's Alex. I was walking past Geronimo McLardy the security guard, when he whispered to me –

"I don't need no brothers to do my busting, I just need the booty to do some cusping". Do you understand, very roughly, what he was saying?

Bob

From: Alexandra
To: Bob Servant
Subject: OK

I do not understand fully about what your friend speaks. It seems to me, that you are frivolous a man. You would like to play only? Where is your photo? What can you offer me to make me love you?

From: Bob Servant
To: Alexandra
Subject: Chill out

Alexandra,
I apologise, let me give you a little more info. I'm Bob Servant and I am

a semi-retired window cleaner from Broughty Ferry. I gave up my round when gypsies nicked my ladders, and I suppose that looking back that was my greatest mistake. But, as you are no doubt aware, I had already done very, very well from the cheeseburger game. I have attached a photo of myself from a recent fishing trip.[9] What do you think? About me, not the fish!!

Bobby Boy xx

From: Alexandra
To: Bob Servant
Subject: A question

The Fish is simply magnificent!:) And it is possible an immodest question? How old are you?

From: Bob Servant
To: Alexandra
Subject: IT WAS A GREAT FISH AND VERY TASTY TOO!

Alexandra,
Thank you for your kind words. That is one of the largest fish I have ever caught. It nearly ripped my bloody arms out. Do you fish much? I used

---

9. This man is not Bob Servant. I have no idea who he is, but the fish looks like a mirror carp.

to nip up to the Monikie reservoir with Frank Theplank. We had some good days. He brought the sandwiches and I brought the beers. But you know what Frank's like, not the brightest, and one time we got there and I whipped out the beers then he whipped out his Tesco bag and inside were his nephew's football boots. I was fucking raging and we never went again. I am 62 years old, but I am as fit as a fiddle.

Bob

From: Alexandra
To: Bob Servant
Subject: Age

It is very a pity, Rob, but it seems that we are not created for one another... To me 23 years, you – 62 years. What prospects of our relations? Let's look at things really. What can you offer me? Your humour?

From: Bob Servant
To: Alexandra
Subject: It's your call monkey face but I do like you!

Alexandra,
One thing before we continue. I see you chose to call me Rob there. I can only hope that this was a one-off as that is one thing that I simply cannot allow. I remember Tommy Peanuts telling me that Bob Wilson beat a jockey half to death live on Grandstand in the early 1980s after the jockey called him Rob[10] and I have to admit that it makes me just as mad. It's Bob or nothing Alexandra, and that's that. You are a frank woman and that is one of the things that I love about you, along with your looks and your admirable interest in big cats. I am looking for a woman, no doubt about it. My success has left me a man of leisure here in Broughty Ferry. I buy supermarket Finest meals, drink premium pints, and often go for the one-man banquet from the Peking Garden even though I will never, ever, finish it.

I have a hell of a lot of cash at my disposal Alexandra. But don't tell the taxman! I have a wonderful house, though it could certainly do with a woman's touch. And I have a fantastic voice, very smoky but also surprisingly gentle. It's your call Alexandra. What I will say is that I think you are beautiful and I am excited about our relationship. I also want children. And believe me – there is lead in this bloody pencil.

Bob x

----

10. There is no record of the former international goalkeeper turned television presenter Bob Wilson ever having physically attacked a jockey, either on or off air.

From: Alexandra
To: Bob Servant
Subject: Hello!

Dear Bob, never Rob!
It was very pleasant to receive from you these answers! You very interesting!

   At leisure I like to look cinema. I like film " Forrest Gump " where a leading role has played Tom Hanks. It is very good film, where many various philosophical ideas and ideas. I also very much like to dance. I could learn to dance you!

   If you want to write to me the letter, my full post address: ████████ ████████████████████████████ Vladivostok, Russian Federation. I think that a meeting is necessary for us! We already can name each other good friends. I am right? I like your sense of humour. I tell my good friends about you,

Alex

From: Bob Servant
To: Alexandra
Subject: LOOSE LIPS COST LIVES

Hello love. It is nice to hear from you but there is something very important I should tell you. Please, Alex, you cannot tell anyone about me. I work for a man called Don Cabbage. He's a bit like Don Corleone, except he's from Broughty Ferry. And his name genuinely is Don. But he's still a gangster. Some of the stuff we get up to is pretty dodgy – selling photocopied disabled parking tickets, homemade jazz mags, and Viagra ice cream (though we've not made any of that yet).

Bob

From: Alexandra
To: Bob Servant
Subject: A secret?

Bob, OK, I understand, that you have secrets in work. I promise to nobody speak about you. But, why it is a secret? You like me more and more. Can we meet New Year together? We shall make a mad act? I can arrive to you. If the idea has liked – answer quickly and we shall discuss details. Your little monkey Alex :)

From: Bob Servant
To: Alexandra
Subject: New Year

Alex,

Merry Christmas![11] You would like to come here, to Broughty Ferry, for New Year? My God, that would be fantastic. I'm not sure what my plans are. Stewpot's Bar is throwing in a finger buffet and a magician and Chappy Williams is having a fancy dress party so we're well covered. I'll have to tidy the house up. Alex, what is your stance on jazz mags? I have probably about 2,000 of the fuckers but I would be willing to bin them if you're going to get on your high horse about the whole thing,

Bob x

From: Alexandra
To: Bob Servant
Subject: Yes, I do!

I want to meet New Year together with you. I have the passport and good friends in a travel company, which can issue the visa. I understand that you are on illegal position and can take cares that your name will not be mentioned.

I can take holiday for 2 months but there is a banal problem. Money. I did not plan trip now. That is I openly speak, that I have no financial opportunity. If you have an opportunity to help me with money then our meeting will be a reality and we can meet New Year together!

Your Alex

From: Bob Servant
To: Alexandra
Subject: OPPORTUNITY AT STEWPOT'S

Alex,

I love the Christmas period, it really shakes things up. I must say, I am delighted by you wanting to come over here for New Year. I think it is a daring decision and I admire that about you Alex. You are a strong, exciting

---

11. This email was indeed sent by Bob on Christmas Day, an impressive dedication to his hobby, and this entire exchange was very intense, with up to a dozen emails a day between Christmas Day and New Year. When I mentioned this to Bob he pointed out that he refuses to watch television at that time of year because of the special festive scheduling (which he describes as 'an insult to his intelligence') and so had a fair amount of time on his hands.

woman who knows when to stand up for herself. You are a fighter Alex, like Rocky Balboa or Martin Luther King. You believe in freedom (your own). I'll tell you what, this old world is a hell of a lot better for having you around.

Alex, I've been thinking of what we will do when you come to live here. I am a man of means, there is absolutely no doubt about that, but I worry you'll be bored with nothing to do other than hang about with old Bob. I was thinking that perhaps you could take a part-time job? Stewpot's Bar has a note up for a lunch waitress. It would only be 12pm-3pm Monday-Saturday with Wednesday off and every other Tuesday being a 2pm finish because of the OAP domino league.

What do you think? I was in there today and mentioned to Terry Darcus the landlord that I had a Russian woman coming over to see me at New Year who might fancy the job but, you know what Terry's like, he just started laughing and walked off.

I've been working on your uniform and I've come up trumps. Nothing too revealing, I'm putting my foot down on that. The last thing I need is you flashing your bits at the boys in Stewpot's. So you can forget that right now or the whole bloody thing's off as far as I'm concerned. I was thinking a t-shirt with 'Bob's Bird' written on the front and 'Stop Looking' on the back?

Bob

From: Alexandra
To: Bob Servant
Subject: Job is not problem

My Darling Bob!
I agree to work some time as the waitress. It would be amusing:) It is valid, it will help me to earn money and in training to English, you are right.

You to me are very interesting and want to see you now! But to issue the visa for such short time, additional financial assets will be necessary. It is necessary for me of 1000 euros that the visa was ready this week. I want to pay for air tickets itself. But money for the visa are necessary already tomorrow!

Yours Alex.

From: Bob Servant
To: Alexandra
Subject: TERRY'S BEING A BASTARD

Alex,
I popped in to see Terry this morning and he said that you have to

fill in an application from. I said I'd vouch for you and he said the last person I vouched for was Frank Theplank, who he employed as a kitchen porter but had to sack after a day when Frank kept sending out meals with carrots carved into nobs. So you have to fill in the form. I tried to talk him round but you know what Terry's like. Send me back the answers as soon as possible and I'll take them in.

WHAT IS YOUR FULL NAME?
AGE?
WHY DO YOU WANT TO WORK IN STEWPOT'S?
WHAT DO YOU THINK YOUR BEST SKILLS ARE?
DO YOU PROMISE NOT TO CARVE CARROTS INTO NOBS?
ARE YOU HONEST?

All the best,

Bob

From: Alexandra
To: Bob Servant
Subject: My Answers for Terry

Dear Bob!
I have just received the letter and I answer your questions.

WHAT IS YOUR FULL NAME?

My full name: the Name: Alexandra the Surname: Dadashov

AGE?

My age: 25 years and 5 months:)

WHY DO YOU WANT TO WORK IN STEWPOT'S?

I want to work during my trip to you to not be to you a burden and consequently, that I like to work, communicate with people. I do not like to idle.

WHAT DO YOU THINK YOUR BEST SKILLS ARE?

I specialize on Russian cuisine more. But I can prepare the Italian and Mexican cuisine also.

DO YOU PROMISE NOT TO CARVE CARROTS INTO NOBS?

:)))) Certainly. But suddenly it clients will want? For me desire of the client – the law:)))

ARE YOU HONEST?

For all time of the life I tried to communicate with people fairly and to
deceive nobody. For me the bitter truth is always better than sweet lie.
Yes, I am fair with you 100%.

So, I hope, that have answered all your questions. Now answer you and
it is maximum fast. When you can send me 1000 euros for the visa?

Alex

From: Bob Servant
To: Alexandra
Subject: Special Russian Riddle Needed

Alex,

I have some news. I spoke to Terry just there but it was absolutely rammed
in Stewpot's because the Dundee United game was on. I tried to speak to
him at half time but I couldn't get near him because he does free sausage
rolls and he got mobbed the minute he came out the kitchen. I was in there
with Tommy Peanuts and he said it was like Beatlemania.

Things calmed down a bit in the second half though so I managed to
have a quick word with him. I told him that you were very interested in the
job and with living with me in Broughty Ferry and him and Tommy started
laughing, I'm not sure what about. I gave him your application form and he
said it looked promising and that he'd look forward to seeing you.

On the way home I bumped into Chappy Williams coming out the
bookies. I said that we wanted to come to his New Year party and he told
me that it's now –

CHAPPY WILLIAM'S SPECIAL NEW YEAR TALENT SHOW

He said that we can only come if we agree to do a special talent act that
lasts at least two minutes. Any ideas? One thought I had was that we could
go to the party as

THE MYSTERIOUS CURTAIN PEOPLE.

We would wear my old curtains over our heads and just cut tiny, tiny slits
into them so we can see where we are going on the way to Chappy's. We
would cut through Forthill because if we walked through the Ferry dressed
as curtains we'd have all sorts of jokers having a pop.

At Chappy's we would wear the curtains and only talk in riddles when
people ask who we are. We could talk in foreign accents. For you this is
easy. I'll probably speak like a Frenchman.

If someone asks me who I am then I'll say –

Oooh, I really don't know
But I do like corn on the cob

If you were to say a name that sounds like this
Then you will have done a good job

What could you say? Do you have a good Russian riddle? It is a fun game, and I need to show Chappy that we have it all worked out. Then we can plan your visa,

Bobby x

From: Alexandra
To: Bob Servant
Subject: a riddle?

Dear Bob!
As I could understand, you require a riddle... That is I should represent the woman whom of other country, but I should not speak, what I from Russia? I have understood?

From: Bob Servant
To: Alexandra
Subject: WE'RE NOT GOING TO GET THE GOLDEN TICKET WITH THAT RUBBISH

Alex,
Come on, we'll have to do better than that. If you stood there in a curtain mumbling about representing women from other country then people would think you were insane.

It is very, very important that we manage to get an invite to Chappy's do. Everyone who is anyone in Broughty Ferry is going to be there and it is a wonderful opportunity to introduce you to local society.

You need a riddle of four lines that says you are from Russia but only through clues.

Bob

From: Alexandra
To: Bob Servant
Subject: Dear Bob!

Dear Bob!
I at last have understood. Ok, but it not last variant:) So...

1. I from the country which knows all world but which nobody understands...
2. I from the country which language hardly is easier, than Chinese:)

3. I from the country, where the most beautiful girls in the world:)
4. I from the country where do not mark Christmas on December, 25:))

You will accept?

Yours Alex

From: Bob Servant
To: Alexandra
Subject: BAD NEWS BUT ALL IS NOT LOST

Alex,

How are you my darling? OK, first the bad news. I finally caught up with Chappy Williams last night at Khan's kebab shop and talked him through your curtains plan.

I told him the riddles and he didn't like the idea at all. He said that they were no good and also pointed out that my old curtains were my Dinosaur ones and everyone would recognise them because I wore them as a poncho for four months when the cheeseburger money came through.

Chappy said we weren't offering enough of an actual talent to take part in the event. He reckons, and I guess he's right, that sticking curtains on your head and speaking in riddles isn't a recognisable talent. I know it seems harsh but Chappy has only got a one-bedroom flat and there has been a lot of interest. I was at Berkeley's Butchers earlier and four of them are going as Bananarama, and I know for a fact that Big Dom Maciocia has put together a Jackson Five from his chip shop.

So, I'm sorry Alex, but the party's off. I still want you to come though. I am confident that you will win the role at Stewpot's and I'm desperate to see you. I want someone who can join me for walks along Broughty Ferry beach, or at the couples only nights at the bowling club, or as medical support and motivator during my monthly crack at the Dawson Park monkey bars record. You, Alex, are that woman.

But first, we need to get a few things straight.

1. Jazz Mags

I have approximately 2,000 jazz mags hidden all over the house. I don't read them that much, but Don Cabbage makes me keep them in case he gets turned over by the police. I give some away, and guys like Frank Theplank and Tommy Peanuts are always borrowing them, but most drawers and cupboards in the house have at least one jazz mag in them. As does the fridge and the freezer. And the oven. And all of my jackets, some of which are lined with them.

Do you want me to clean up the jazz mags into one, easily monitored pile? You could maybe limit me to one mag a week, or maybe I could only be allowed to read them if you were out with the girls for a glass of wine, or in hospital having been run over. What do you think?

2. Apron

I have a novelty apron I wear when I am making dinner, and some other times too. It makes it look as if I have a women's body and am wearing a brassiere and women's pants. Is this acceptable?

3. Cartoon

A few months ago, Archie Campbell won the bowling club's monthly Saucy Cartoon Competition[12] with something he got off the Internet. It was a typical stunt by Archie, all flash and showing off, so I told him it was rubbish and not as funny as Garfield in the Dundee Courier. But the thing was, Alex, that the cartoon is actually very funny indeed. When Archie wasn't looking, I popped it in my pocket and stuck it up on the kitchen wall when I got home.

Basically it's a job interview and the man says 'so you can't keep a secret, well you've still got the job' to this woman. It's funny because keeping secrets is important but, here's the thing, the woman's bazookas are hanging out! So he gives her the job anyway!

It cracks me up and having it in the kitchen is a good way of starting the day with a smile.

What do you think? Do you see this as a bit of fun or are you going to get all angry and say it's not fair on the woman even though she's just a cartoon woman? Maybe you'd rather have a photo of babies up in the kitchen, or a calendar so you can mark up when you're going to the barbers?

Let me know what you think about these things please Alex, so I can start getting things ready for you here.

Bob x

From: Alexandra
To: Bob Servant
Subject: Money for visa needed now

My darling Bob!
I shall answer your questions. But if I shall not pay the money today then I cannot receive the visa! You understand?

1. It is not necessary for you "to clean up the jazz mags into one, easily monitored pile". As I have understood, jazz mags is a part of your life which you very much value. What for to pretend to someone to anothers?

---

12. No bowling club in the Broughty Ferry area admits to holding such an event.

So leave like you have usually.

2. Mmm. This threat looks sexually:) To me is not a problem to carry it:)

3. To me too it is very interesting Cartoon. I find it amusing and I hope, that when we shall be together we shall cheerfully look at it together:)

I hope, that have answered all your questions. Now I shall tell you cost has increased to 1300 euro because additional expenses for renewal of documents are required. You should inform me when you can send me this sum. And tell me what airport I should come to? Do you like photo I send to show my love?

Alex

From: Bob Servant
To: Alexandra
Subject: WHAT A CLEVER PHOTO!

Hello Alex,
What a clever photo! At first I thought it was just you blowing old Bob a kiss and then I looked at the computer screen and there was old Bob himself! Great stuff. A nice idea, well executed. I think it's probably best that you fly to Edinburgh airport. I can get Geronimo McLardy to drive me there to pick

you up. He'll do it for jazz mags. Oh, what a wonderful day that will be!

When the bank opens I am going to ask for the money for your visa. To hell with the cost!

Love,

Bob

From: Alexandra
To: Bob Servant
Subject: Visa

Hello Bob,
Once again the information on how you should send the money –

1. Name of the addressee: Alexandra
2. Surname of the addressee: Dadashov
3. City and country of the addressee: Vladivostok, Russia

I hope, that you can make it in the nearest hour because our banks work only up to 3 PM.

Alex

From: Bob Servant
To: Alexandra
Subject: THE HEAT IS ON

Alex,
I have had a terrible day. This morning, Don Cabbage turned up and said I owed him money so he was going to live in my house for a while. I have had to cook for him and pour him drinks and all he does is laugh and ruffle my hair really hard. Don has one thing he does called 'The Angry Dove'. He twists his hands together and kind of waggles them like wings and says 'Oh, oh, the dove's getting angry' and then attacks you with the dove. Well, not the dove, with his hands. He punches you in the face, basically, with the dove's wings. Well, they're not the dove's wings. They're his fists.

What should I do Alex? I am scared and frightened and it seems like my whole world is collapsing onto my knees and shins. Sometimes I wish I had never got involved with Don Cabbage and a life of crime for the last couple of years. Yes, it's given me a lot, but it has also taken away a lot and now Don Cabbage is living here, in my house.

Please write back soon. I am too scared to check the email when he is around but whenever he naps I will sneak over and check.

Bob

From: Alexandra
To: Bob Servant
Subject: We have no time for this!

My darling Bob! I was bothered with this. I lose time, money and
patience. The question on my reception of the visa is solved tomorrow.
If you will not send me money our meeting will be unreal because
the embassy will not give me the visa. Really for you it is difficult to
understand it? If for you money not a problem why you cannot make it
now or tomorrow? To me has bothered to waste time, money and my
reputation. You still have time and we can be together.

Alex

From: Bob Servant
To: Alexandra
Subject: I AM TRYING MY BEST FOR GOD'S SAKE

Alex,
I am trying my darling but it is very hard for me with Don Cabbage being in
the house all the time. He is a very scary man. I have some money here,
around £5,000 but I do not want him to know I have this money do you
see? Once he leaves I can go and send it to you from the Post Office.

Earlier, Don Cabbage went to the bathroom and I went to look in his
room. He has some bad things in there Alex, including an axe and some
really big potatoes that I think he uses as missiles. I am very scared Alex,
what should I do? As soon as he leaves I can send you the £5,000. Please
write back and please understand, I love you but my life is in danger from
Don Cabbage,

Bob xx

From: Alexandra
To: Bob Servant
Subject: We have not much time

Darling Bob
I know you are scared but I am already tired to wait for hours with you of
a meeting. You must be quick,

Alex

From: Bob Servant
To: Alexandra
Subject: WONDERFUL NEWS

Alex,

I have some fantastic news. Don Cabbage has left! He said that someone in Lochee owed him £15 for some jazz mags and he went off to get him. He says that if I keep my nose clean then he'll leave me alone for a while. Thank God for that!

So we're back on track! I have the money here to make our dreams come true! How quickly could you be here? I have a surprise for you. I have bought something that I think you will like. I will give you a clue. You need to feed it. Can you guess?

Bob

From: Alexandra
To: Bob Servant
Subject: Hello

Bob!

I did not want to lose good relations with my friends in a travel company. I have already informed you, how you can help me. You can have a way to any branch Western Union. I have made all for this purpose. If you will not help me, I shall be compelled to give in parts 1300 euro to my friends within several months. I think now that you play with me?

Yours Alex

From: Bob Servant
To: Alexandra
Subject: OH COME ON ALEX, DON'T BE LIKE THAT!

Alex,

What kind of weirdo would spend all this time emailing you if they were not serious? I have the money to send to the Western Union in Vladivostok but what is the point in sending you money when you are suggesting that I am some sort of joker? I have even bought you a present, it was supposed to be surprise, but maybe if you see it then you will understand that I am serious.

Yours in hope,

Bob x

From: Alexandra
To: Bob Servant
Subject: I am sorry

My dear Bob!
I am sorry for behaviour. I am very tired... I very much want to be with you. You should understand, that for me it is very difficult to accept again the man. But you have very much liked me, I do not hide it. And now I shall be very glad, if our meeting with you will take place. I wait for concrete actions. I am very much intrigued with a gift which you have prepared me?

Alex

From: Bob Servant
To: Alexandra
Subject: READY?

Alex,
Ok, apology accepted. Are you ready to see your present?

Bob x

From: Alexandra
To: Bob Servant
Subject: Yes!

Yes, certainly, I am ready to see my present:))

From: Bob Servant
To: Alexandra
Subject: HERE WE GO! HE'S CALLED CHAMPION!

From: Alexandra
To: Bob Servant
Subject: I like it

My dear Bob!
Your gift has very much liked me, very originally. Still anybody similar
in life did not give anything to me. Now about our affairs. I very much
hope, that today you will make that for a long time promised me . . . to
Western Union! I expect your answer...

Alex

From: Bob Servant
To: Alexandra
Subject: NOT LONG NOW!

Alex,

I am so excited that you like your present. I was going to Carnoustie on the
bus the other day when I spotted Champion in a field. 'Aye, aye', I thought,
'What's going on over there then?' So I got off the bus and went to have a
good look at the blighter.

Now, Alex, just about every household in Carnoustie owns at least one
ostrich[13] but for some reason the farmer hadn't shifted Champion. The next
thing you know we'd shaken hands on me to take Champion off his hands
for £150, eight jazz mags and the spice rack I won in the bowling club
Christmas raffle.

So tomorrow I'm going to get up, have a quick bite to eat at Stewpot's
Bar and a couple of liveners, then nip up to Carnoustie on the bus and
pick up Champion. Then I'll come back here, tie him up in the garden and
race round to the Post Office to send the cash. Are you looking forward to
seeing me and Champion?

Also, do you have any idea what I should feed Champion? Would he
eat chips?

Bob x

---

13. Although no exact measure can be given (you do not need a licence to
purchase an ostrich, which I found surprising) a quick check with local RSPCA
officials suggests that this claim is untrue.

From: Alexandra
To: Bob Servant
Subject: Let us resolve this today now

Send the money as the most important part of your travels tomorrow. Certainly, I very much wait happily for our meeting. It will be better, if to my arrival the Champion will be little bit hungry then I could feed him:) Chips? He loves chips? I never saw ostriches earlier, it is very interesting to me:))

Now I wait from you for the information on a remittance that I could continue the preparation to be with you and Champion.

Alex

From: Bob Servant
To: Alexandra
Subject: A rollercoaster of a day

Alex,

An unforgettable day. I went along to Stewpot's first thing and told all the boys I was off to pick up an ostrich for my Russian girlfriend and they were giving it, 'Oh aye, your Russian girlfriend Bob, is that the one that's going to work here?' and I was saying 'Yeah, that's her, Alexandra' and they all started laughing.

So it was a good atmosphere and then they started saying that Russian men can drink a bottle of vodka straight and if I couldn't do that then you would leave me. Well, I wasn't going to risk that so I told Terry to line me up his best bottle and a couple of cheese sandwiches.

Now, I'm a drinker Alex, I've never hidden that from you but I have two Achilles heels. The first is strong women and the second is vodka. They just don't agree with me and after an hour or so it all got a bit blurry. Then suddenly I was alert again but someone had stolen one of my sandwiches so I went round the pub asking who had my sandwich but people just kept laughing.

Then Terry told me to look in the mirror behind the bar and I saw that the sandwich was stuck to my forehead. I must have fallen asleep onto it or something. So I took the sandwich off and left Stewpot's in the huff and went to catch the bus to Carnoustie.

It was quite hard because my legs weren't working properly but I got on the bus OK and then gave everyone a laugh with some animal jokes and a bit of a sing.

I got off the bus fine though I did fall into a hedge. When I found Champion he was in great form. I didn't have a lead so I took off my jumper and stuck it over his head and used a sleeve to lead him out back to the bus stop. I was feeding him some pork scratchings when the farmer appeared and went absolutely berserk.

He was saying stuff like, 'what the fuck do you think you're playing at?' 'get that fucking jumper off it's head' and 'you're a fucking basket case and I'm going to call the police'.

I kept my dignity and ignored him and he went off to get the police, but then the bus came. The driver must have been texting his mate or something because he actually stopped and I had Champion halfway on before he even noticed. He got scared and said there was no way I could bring an ostrich on the bus and I said to just charge him half fare but then the other people on the bus started getting involved (even though it was none of their business) and were all screaming and stuff.

Of course, that set Champion off who went totally bananas, lashing out with his feet and pecking away. He lifted a woman's bunnet clean off and caught a man with a moustache an absolute beauty on the side of the head. 'That's one peck on the cheek you didn't ask for!' I said, to lighten the mood but the guy didn't get it, he just rolled about holding his head and swearing at me.

Then the police turned up and so I went to have a wee chat with them but tripped and went into another hedge. I don't remember much after that, just the police standing about and then Champion being led off by the farmer. I shouted 'See you later Champion, you can keep the jumper' but he didn't reply.

The policemen brought me home and said I might get done for cruelty and fined, so I might need that money that I was going to use for your visa. I'm sorry about Champion but, to be honest, I don't think it's safe to have a family pet that could go off the handle like that.

And, anyway, all is not lost! I went to Doc Ferry's bar to have a think about things and bumped into Chappy Williams. I told him what happened and he said he had something in the car I could have. He went off and came back with a bloody dog! I couldn't believe it. Chappy had really red cheeks and was out of breath but seemed to find everything very funny. I asked what it was called and he said 'Bob' so I said, 'But that's my name' and he said that I should call it 'Bob the Dog' so I don't get confused.

It was hard walking home with Bob, he didn't seem to be listening to anything I said but we're back now and I think he's sleeping. I'm sorry about the money thing but I hope that you can maybe come over here using your own money and I'll pay for the groceries. And the food for Bob. Bob the Dog I mean, not me.

Love,

Bob. Not Bob the Dog! He wouldn't be able to write!

From: Alexandra
To: Bob Servant
Subject: Re: a rollercoaster of a day

Fuck you! To me has bothered to read your delirium

No Reply

4
Uncle Bob's African Adventure

From: Joseph Udeze
To: Bob Servant
Subject: Are you interested?

Dear Good Friend,
I am Joseph Udeze, solicitor at law. I am the personal Attorney To Mr
Christian Clark, a national of your country, who lived in Nigeria. In May
2000, my client was killed in a car accident in Kano. The bank where he
had an account of $9.5m has issued me a notice to provide the beneficiary
or have the account confiscated within 20 days.

Since I have been unsuccessful in locating the relatives, I now seek
your consent to present you as the beneficiary of the $9.5m. If you agree,
we can discuss your percentage. Please i will like you to send to me
your full name and address, private telephone and fax number for easy
communication.

Best regards,

Barr. Joseph Udeze (Esq.)

From: Bob Servant
To: Joseph Udeze
Subject: Good morning

Joseph,
I cannot help you with the Clarky stuff, but if you can prove that you
live in Africa then I have a business proposal for you,

Your Servant,

Bob Servant

From: Joseph Udeze
To: Bob Servant
Subject: FURTHER DETAILS

Dear Bob,
Yes! I live in Africa and as such would be ready for your proposal.

Thanks,

Joseph

From: Bob Servant
To: Joseph Udeze
Subject: Now we're talking...

Joseph,

Listen my new pal, I have an idea that I would like to run past you. I think, and hope, that it will blow your socks off. I have a small cafe here in Broughty Ferry. We mostly work off the taxi drivers and posties, you know the drill – sausages (link and square), bacon rolls, meths. You'd be amazed at the meths we shift Joseph. Around half the posties that work out of Dundee East Sorting Office are on the meths day and night. I heard from Tommy Peanuts that a couple of them actually get paid in meths.[14]

Anyway, to cut a long story short, I want to give the cafe a total overhaul. I'm happy to close the place down for two weeks and really go to town on it.

What I'm thinking is this –

UNCLE BOB'S AFRICAN ADVENTURE

I would fill the place with plants and trees and make it really dark. When people came in they would literally have to trek to the counter, using a machete to get through the vines and avoid being attacked by the lions. These would be large paper mache lion heads that I would wear, popping up from behind the foliage and roaring in their ears.

Let me know if you think you could help,

Yours,

Bob

From: Joseph Udeze
To: Bob Servant
Subject: I am waiting...

Dear Bob,

Nice talks...I shall be willing to render assistance if you can give to me

---

14. This pair of claims is, quite obviously, complete nonsense. Not only does the Royal Mail's Dundee East Sorting Office have no record of methylated spirits addiction, the theory that any of the postmen there would be paid using methylated spirits is entirely inaccurate and, indeed, ludicrous.

further details. You have made a nice catch! How can I help with this enterprise?

Thanks,

Joseph.

\-

From: Bob Servant
To: Joseph Udeze
Subject: What I need

Joseph,
That is great news. What I need is this - an African team that can come up with sizzling African dishes that the cafe can cook. And, fuck me Joseph, I need it now. What do you think? I would need full recipes and would be willing to pay $500 for each one. Right now, I urgently need two genuine African recipes for which I will pay $1,000 by Western Union.

I need –

The name of the dish
The ingredients needed
Instructions for cooking

I am incredibly excited about this. I am going to close the cafe next week and start the work on it.

Yours,

Bob Servant

\-

From: Joseph Udeze
To: Bob Servant
Subject: OK

Dear Bob,
I have just read your mail, and I am sure that gradually I understand what you are talking about. All is well and like I assured you before now, I can do that for you. Africa as continent has a lot of dishes, but if I am to get correct answers to your request, then I have to concentrate on Nigerian dishes which I am very familiar with. I shall be responding further in that regards. Thanks for consulting me!

Joseph.

\-

From: Bob Servant
To: Joseph Udeze
Subject: An announcement

Joseph,
I hereby appoint you –

HEAD OF MENU CONSULTATION at UNCLE BOB'S AFRICAN
ADVENTURE.

That's right, you've got it. I have given you an opportunity Joseph, do not
let me down,

Uncle Bob

From: Joseph Udeze
To: Bob Servant
Subject: My true position on the matter

Dear Bob,
I have read your mail this morning and it is my sincere wish to help
you. Like I stated, I am a lawyer by profession and as such would want
to handle any transaction that I am having with anybody legally so that
we don't end up misunderstanding ourselves. Before we can commence
actions please forward your full personal details.

Meanwhile I have consulted a specialist in Food Technology and that
is to give to you the best of satisfaction in your demand. An investment
has to be made and that is why I need to be assured that you would not let
me down because as a professional in that field, I am required to pay to
him consultation fees. Let me know your considerations over this.

Thanks and I am wishing you a successful endeavour.

Joseph U.

From: Bob Servant
To: Joseph Udeze
Subject: Sounds good

Joseph,
Good to hear from you my friend. Things are coming along really well here.
Old Joan, who works behind the counter, has taken it upon herself to start
learning Swahili, which is a lovely touch. I think she was worried that I was
going to sack her and get in someone younger and more exotic when we
reopen and it's great to see the staff on their toes like this.

I have a very, very good feeling about UNCLE BOB'S AFRICAN
ADVENTURE. I think we are going to wipe the floor with the competition,

in particular ARCHIE'S PIT STOP. Archie and I used to be friends until one night a few years ago. We were at the bowling club getting pissed up and I stupidly told Archie how well my cafe was doing.

He'd just got £20,000 redundancy from the Michelin and the next thing you know the bastard has opened up ARCHIE'S PIT STOP one hundred yards down the road from the cafe. We've never spoken since and I hope that I drive him to the wall. By Christ, he'll near enough shit himself when he sees UNCLE BOB'S AFRICAN ADVENTURE. I can't wait.

That is great news about the food technician. He sounds just the calibre of person that we need to get on board. Please welcome him to the team from me.

Also, here's the other info you need –

I'm single/available

Cafe address –

Uncle Bob's Wonderful Cafe
71 The High Street
███████████

Dundee,
Scotland UK

Look forward to hearing from you my friend. How long until the first recipe? Have some fun with it Joseph - surprise me and tease me, feel free to sauce it up, but not too spicy please.

Uncle Bob

From: Joseph Udeze
To: Bob Servant
Subject: Have a look at the attached files

Dear Bob,
I have read your mail and also saw your information. I am still wanting to know your age. Thanks for all the information which has given me more confidence in what we are about doing. As I promised you in my early morning mail, I have attached here scanned copies of my own photographs for your perusal.[15]

Thanks,

Joseph.

---

15. Mr Udeze also provided a family photo which has been removed for legal reasons.

From: Bob Servant
To: Joseph Udeze
Subject: Sensational

Joseph,

Thank you so much for sending me these photos. They are simply sensational. In the first one you look extremely smart and have really turned yourself out nicely. In the second, you have been captured brilliantly relaxing with your family. The photos, if you like, show the two sides of Joseph Udeze, am I correct?

You look quite like Sir Trevor MacDonald, who used to read the news over here and play for Newcastle United.[16] Is he a relation of yours?

Thank you,

Bob

PS I am 62 years old.

----

16. I can only speculate that this is a weak joke aimed at Newcastle United's 1970s centre forward Malcolm 'Supermac' Macdonald. The newscaster and television presenter Sir Trevor MacDonald has, quite evidently, never played professional football.

From: Joseph Udeze
To: Bob Servant
Subject: Thanks for your words

Dear Bob,
All is well, thanks for your words. I shall be getting to you tomorrow further information as soon as I have spoken with the food specialist. Just relax your mind because I am working things out in a way that favors everybody.

I have just viewed a picture on the web of Sir Trevor MacDonald and I am not related. People can resemble each other and that is exactly what you have spotted. I don't think I have any relation over there in Scotland.

Have a nice time.

Yours truly,

Joseph U.

From: Bob Servant
To: Joseph Udeze
Subject: Frank

Joseph,
Hello my friend, good to hear from you and don't worry about the Sir Trevor MacDonald thing, it doesn't affect your employment. Joseph, I really need to get these recipes in as my chef Frank Theplank has to start practising very soon so that he can cook them by the time the cafe opens.

Frank is not the sharpest knife in the box and he is already bloody furious with the African theme, so I am keen to get him working on them asap. I will get Frank to email you directly. Please send the recipes straight to him to save time and then email me to arrange payment.

Many thanks,

Uncle Bob

From: Frank Theplank
To: Joseph Udeze
Subject: RECIPES

HULLO
I AM THE CHEF AT BOB SERVANT'S CAFE AND HE TOLD ME TO
EMAIL YOU AND ASK FOR THE AFRICAN RECIPES WHICH YOU ARE
SENDING US FOR THIS STUPID NEW AFRICAN CAFE HE IS MAKING

FRANK THEPLANK

From: Joseph Udeze
To: Bob Servant, Frank Theplank
Subject: From the chef

Forwarded Message –

From: Christian Bala
To: Joseph Udeze
Subject: African Menu

ATTN: MR. BOB SERVANT /FRANK THEPLANK,
I AM CHRISTIAN BALA (CHEF). HAVING RECEIVED
INSTRUCTIONS FROM MR. JOSEPH UDEZE, I WILL OUTLINE
SOME OF THE POPULAR AFRICAN DISHES. I SHALL ALSO
BE WILLING TO BRIEF YOU FURTHER ON HOW THEY ARE
PREPARED TO GET THE BEST OF TASTE AS SOON AS WE HAVE
AGREED TERMS.

BELOW ARE SOME FOR THE MOMENT:-

1) ABACHA (AFRICAN SALAD)

INGREDIENTS: - CASSAVA (SHREDED), UGBA (OIL BEAN),
PALM OIL, CRAYFISH, GARDEN EGG, HERRING FISH, COW
HIDE (KPOMO), UKAZI LEAF, SALT/PEPPER.

2) YAM PORRIDGE.

INGREDIENTS: - YAM, PALM OIL, CRAY FISH OR SHRIMPS,
PEPPER, GREEN LEAF OR PUMPKIN VEGETABLE, WATER LEAF,
SMOKED FISH, SALT.

3) UGBA (OIL BEAN)

INGREDIENTS: - OIL BEAN (SHREDED), STOCKFISH, PALM OIL,
CRAYFISH (GRINDED), CRABS, PEPPER, POTASH, SALT.

4) ISI EWU (GOAT HEAD)

INGREDIENTS: - GOAT HEAD, PALM OIL (RED), CENT LEAF
(NCHANWU), POTASH, GREEN PEPPER, SALT, OIL BEAN (UGBA)

5) AFANG SOUP.

INGREDIENTS: - WATER LEAF, OKAZI LEAF, BEEF/FISH,
PERIWINKLE, SNAILS, CRABS, PALM OIL, PEPPER, SALT.

I SHALL BE WAITING FOR YOUR COMMENTS.

CHRISTIAN BALA

From: Bob Servant
To: Joseph Udeze, Christian Bala, Frank Theplank
Subject: MENU

Joseph/Michael,
Good news, the cafe is coming on brilliantly and UNCLE BOB'S AFRICAN
ADVENTURE is really starting to take shape. I am trying to get hold of a
camel and have put an advert for one in the window at Toshy's Hardware.
Once Frank has got your dishes nailed we're going to be in business. I
have chosen 3 dishes below, send the full instructions to Frank Theplank,

Bob

YAM PORRIDGE

ISI EWU

AFANG SOUP

From: Christian Bala
To: Bob Servant, Joseph Udeze, Frank Theplank
Subject: More on African Menu

ATTN: MR. BOB SERVANT /FRANK THEPLANK, EVERYTHING
WILL BE AS YOU DESIRE. I AM WORKING OUT MODALITIES
WITH JOSEPH TO FIGURE OUT THE MOST EXCELLENT WAYS
TO DELIVER THE INSTRUCTIONS SO THAT YOU DO NOT MAKE
MISTAKES.
    I WANT YOU TO JUST COUNT ON ME FOR A SUCCESSFUL
"UNCLE BOB'S AFRICAN ADVENTURE" THAT WILL CAUSE
TRAFFIC-JAM (HOLDUP OR GO-SLOW) IN SCOTLAND. WE ARE
ALSO WISHING TO KNOW HOW MUCH YOU INTEND TO PAY US
FOR THE SERVICES WE HAVE DESIRED TO RENDER?

THANKS,

CHRISTIAN BALA

From: Frank Theplank
To: Bob Servant, Joseph Udeze, Christian Bala
Subject: Yam

IS YAM JUST AFRICAN FOR HAM?

From: Bob Servant
To: Frank Theplank, Joseph Udeze, Christian Bala
Subject: Appointments

Hello everyone,

Firstly, some official appointments. I think this is the best structure for you guys over there (or 'The Recipe Boys', as I like to call you when talking to Old Joan), and us cats here in Broughty Ferry. So here's the lowdown –

Joseph Udeze - Menu Consultant
Christian Bala - Food Technician
Frank Theplank – Head Chef
Bob Servant – Owner and Inspiration/Father Figure
Old Joan – Cashier

NB Joseph Udeze and Christian Bala also can be collectively referred to as 'The Recipe Boys'. (as long as they're OK with that)

What do you think? With this team we will not only stop traffic, as you say, but blast Archie's Pit Stop into oblivion. Send the recipes to Frank Theplank today. He will check them over. If everything is fine then I will pay you $500 each recipe and then order some more immediately. So get your thinking caps on Recipe Boys!

The cafe is now closed and undergoing refurbishment. I am going down to Homebase this afternoon to buy the foliage for the jungle theme and I'm going to pop into Remnant Kings and see if they have much in the way of animal skins.

Uncle Bob

PS Frank, yam is not ham. I will explain more this afternoon.

From: Christian Bala
To: Bob Servant, Frank Theplank
Subject: AFRICAN MENU (The Yam Potage)

MENU NO: (1) THE YAM POTAGE,

INGREDIENTS: --- YAM, PALM OIL, CRAY FISH OR SHRIMPS, PEPPER, ONION, CENT LEAF, GREEN LEAF OR PUMPKIN LEAF, WATER LEAF, SMOKED FISH, SALT ETC.

HOW TO PREPARE YAM POTAGE: --- PEEL YAM - CUT INTO CUBES, WASH AND PUT IN POT. ADD WATER THAT COVERS THE YAM. ADD PALM OIL AND BOIL THEN PLACE ON BURNER

(STOVE, GAS COOKER E.T.C). BOIL FOR 5 MINUTES THEN INTRODUCE SPICES SUCH AS CHOPPED ONIONS, CENT LEAF (NCHANWU) TO GIVE YAM POTAGE FLAVOR, GRINDED PEPPER AND CRAY FISH OR SHRIMPS. THEN ADD SMOKED FISH AND OTHER VEGETABLES AND BOIL UNTIL YAM IS READY FOR EATING.

HOW TO SERVE YAM POTAGE: -- NORMALLY SERVED HOT IN TWO DIFFERENT BOWLS - BOILED YAM IN ONE PLATE WITH BROTH (SOUP) IN OTHER. A SET OF CUTLERIES (KNIFE, SPOON AND FORK) IS USED TO EAT YAM POTAGE.

ENJOY YOUR MEAL! THIS IS JUST THE TIP OF THE ICEBERG! I SHALL BE WAITING FOR YOUR COMMENTS,

CHRISTIAN BALA (CHEF).

From: Bob Servant
To: Christian Bala, Joseph Udeze
Subject: The Yam Potage

Christian,

Thank you very much for this recipe. Frank is not working today as he trapped his foot in a drain on the way home last night and is unable to walk. With anyone else I would find this suspicious but, with Frank, I believe it. The guy is a complete fool. However, he is a good chef and I can't wait to see how he does with these recipes.

Can you please send us the other two recipes today? Then I can get Frank to cook all three tomorrow when he comes in. Once he's done that, and assuming that they are as delicious as they sound, then I will order more and pay you for the three.

I attach a photo of Frank.[17] It's important you know what the Scottish gang looks like over there at Recipe HQ. Also, I'm going to start hunting about for a lion's head. Should I get a male or female? I know the easy answer is male but sometimes I think female lions are more scary because you wouldn't expect it from them. I don't want one that's too scary though as it would be disastrous if I were to give someone a heart attack. Maybe I'll just wear a normal tracksuit with the lion's head so they realise it is not a real lion,

Bob

---

17. This is not Frank The Plank, and no negative conclusions should be drawn about this man. If anything, he looks like a fine man.

From: Christian Bala
To: Bob Servant
Subject: Payment

Dear Bob,
You will be fine with male or female lion head as people will be terrified of both. Your cafe will be a big success. We are ever willing to render every services that you desired, but would not do so unprofessionally.

We have released the information on how to prepare Yam Potage as a sample of what we are capable of doing. We are also willing to release the other two menus but it is our wish to demand for at least an advance payment to proceed with the assignment which we are very willing to accomplish. Your good understanding would be highly appreciated.

Thanks,

Christian Bala

From: Bob Servant
To: Christian Bala, Joseph Udeze
Subject: Bad news

Gentlemen,
I have bad news. Archie, that idiot, has been coming round the last couple of days and winding up Frank and myself. I take him with a pinch of salt but unfortunately Frank gets very angry with the teasing. Archie keeps tricking Frank by making him say words that he says are African but really they are just bad words spelt backwards. You know, the usual - DRATSAB, and so on.

Anyway, yesterday he really went to town on Frank when I was up at the bank sorting out some change. I came back in and Frank was wearing a lion outfit that had been superglued up the back. Archie had told him it would help him cook African food and then glued him into it. Poor Frank was absolutely roasting, still trying to make that Yam Potage but it was very hard for him as he could hardly see out the eyeholes. Also, a group of local children saw him through the window and came in and started throwing things at him.

When I arrived I saw one hit him on the head and another jab him in the bottom with a rolling pin. Actually, the guy who did that was in his late 40s. I told him I could understand the kids messing about but it was a bit much him getting involved. He apologised and said he had been attracted in from the street by the kids laughing and found himself getting sucked into the whole thing.

I managed to clear everyone out but Frank was absolutely livid. I got the suit off and he just sat there, rocking on a chair, saying 'Pit stop, Pit stop' over and over. I didn't know what to say. I told him to take the rest of the day off and he just got up, smiled and said, 'Goodbye Bob. I'll take care of it'. The funny thing is that he looked so peaceful when he left.

I got on with work (I've been trying to draw palm trees on the wall but they just look like big seagulls) and then a couple of hours later I heard sirens. I ran down the street just in time to see Frank dancing in the flames of what used to be ARCHIE'S PIT STOP, wearing the lion outfit.

There was nothing I could do and the police were there immediately and carted him off. As he passed me he shouted, "Say goodbye to the Recipe Boys" before they dragged him off. There was something strange about him though, and it was only when I looked closer that I noticed the lion outfit had some form of liquid all over it.

Frank was covered, you've guessed it, in Yam Potage.

Of course, there's no way I can continue with the business now. Frank was a wonderful chef and, in many ways, was also my rock. I am going to sell up and go back into window cleaning. Thank you so much for all your work, it's just lucky that it wasn't wasted.

All the very best for the future,

Bob Servant

From: Christian Bala
To: Bob Servant

YOU ARE A STUPID MAN

No Reply

5

The Sea Could Not Take Him, No Woman Could Tame Him

From: Colin Jackson
To: Bob Servant
Subject: Job Offer

Good Day,

My name is Mr Colin Jackson an artist in the United Kingdom. I have been selling my art works for the last 3 years to galleries and private collectors all around the world but am always facing serious difficulties as people are always offering to pay with financial instruments that I am not familiar with.

I undergo so much difficulty in converting them to cash and am currently in search of a representative who I am willing to pay 15% each transaction. You would receive payments, convert them to cash, deduct 15% and send the remaining funds to me. If you have read and understood my offer, please indicate your willingness to work for me.

Best Regards

Colin Jackson

From: Bob Servant
To: Colin Jackson
Subject: I would love to see your work?

Colin,

Thank you for getting in touch and for thinking of old Bobby boy for this unique proposal. You sound like a fine fellow and well done on sticking with your art. So many creative folk give up at the first hurdle and it is really heartening that you have swum against the tide. Could you possibly email me some examples of your work? I am currently looking to redecorate and maybe they could be just the ticket!

Your Servant,

Bob Servant

From: Colin Jackson
To: Bob Servant
Subject: Here you go Bob

Hello Bob,

Thanks for getting back to me, i really appreciate you taking your time to reply to my job offer and also being interested in working with me as a business partner. I have attached a picture of my artwork as you asked, hope you will love it and it becomes my ticket lol!

Actually why i need you is as a cashier where you take out your percentage as agreed from every payment. Since you the first person to respond to my offer then I will consider you as my first choice of cashier which am going to give a trial? The information i will require from you will be

Your Full Name
Full Address
Contact Phone

Next we will talk about banking details. Hope everything is being understood here, waiting to hear from you.

Colin Jackson

From: Bob Servant
To: Colin Jackson
Subject: You have an exceptional talent

Colin,
Thank you so much for sending that example, which is a stunning piece. I've always been a plum fan and, I must say, I had a hunch that you would be too. I love art Colin, and I always have, but it's hard being an art lover here in Broughty Ferry. Frank Theplank once told me that his favourite artist is Rolf Harris and I know for a fact that he wasn't joking. I don't have much time for Harris since he shot that dog on the telly.[18]

I would love to buy some of your art Colin. There you go, I've said it. I don't have much in the house and I think that sticking a few paintings up would really brighten up the joint as well as being a big hit with any skirt that comes round.

---

18. Bob is presumably referring, erroneously, to a 1994 edition of *Animal Hospital*, presented by Rolf Harris, where a German Shepherd called Floss was put down on medical grounds. Far from being involved in the dog's death, Harris was visibly upset by the incident.

Do you have any paintings of ships? I live right beside the river Tay and I often sit in the garden, especially in the summer, drinking cider and watch the boats messing about out there. I think it would be great to have a few boats on the walls in the house. There's another reason as well for me wanting a boat painting, to be honest, but I'm a little embarrassed to say.

Hope you're having a nice weekend. It's raining cats and dogs here. Good weather for ducks!

Bob

From: Colin Jackson
To: Bob Servant
Subject: Thank You

Thanks Bob,
It's a pleasure hearing from you, I am truly flattered. I have not many paintings of ships but I do have one that is below.[19] Do you like it? Let me know what you think and also if you are still going to work with me as a cashier or a customer? It is a cashier I need but I will not turn down a customer! lol sounds funny Bob.

Thanks again for your mail looking for your reply.

Colin

From: Bob Servant
To: Colin Jackson
Subject: A Proposition

Colin,
That is absolutely enchanting - a sleepy harbour scene on a summer's morning, if I may be so bold! It is so life-like Colin, I feel like stripping naked and diving through my computer screen into the water, though I'm so drunk I'd probably miss and end up wedged in the bin. That would be just my bloody luck.

I would prefer a slightly different painting. As I touched on before, there is something else I should tell you. You see, Colin, I used to be in the Merchant Navy. It was during my wilderness years before I hit the glory days of the cheeseburger vans. That much is true but in actual fact I never set foot on a boat.

---

19. At this point Mr Jackson provided a wonderful photo of a harbour scene but the image was badly corrupted. When I informed Bob of this he responded that he had some photos at home that were 'a lot more corrupt than that'. This was an observation that Bob found so amusing I momentarily thought he might choke to death on his sandwich.

I was dismissed after two weeks' training for a misunderstanding. On our last lesson a female instructor was talking us through some First Aid. With it being the last day, spirits were running high and one thing led to another and I put my hand up the instructor's skirt. It was just a bit of harmless fun Colin (I only waved it about up there to get some laughs, no funny business), and this was the late 1970s so you'd think it would have all blown over but the fuckers said it was out of order and kicked me out.[20]

Anyway, when I talk to the boys in the bars of Broughty Ferry I have occasionally exaggerated my Merchant Navy career. I've told them all sorts - that I captained my own ship called 'Bob's Beauty', that I had a Chinese wife and that I once knocked out a shark off the coast of Jamaica with a head butt.

What I would love is a painting where there is a man in quite a big boat but you can't see his face? Then I could say that it is a painting of me in 'Bob's Beauty' from the late 1970s. Maybe you could paint some flares on the man. What do you think? I have a fair bit of money stashed away for situations like this, which arise a lot more than you'd expect.

Bob Servant

From: Colin Jackson
To: Bob Servant
Subject: I could do this

Ok Bob,

Really a funny story bob, what you are asking for is not impossible i can do it for you, with your name printed on it like you said 'Bob's Beauty' but its going to cost you quite a lot of money for such a thing.

It is not a problem for me but you have to pay part of the money in advance to assure me that you will pick it up so my effort won't be wasted. so if you wish then send me the following –

Your picture that you will like to see on the painting

The color combination that you wish

The advance of $1000 then the balance of $1500 when your painting gets to you

---

20. I think, for Bob's sake, I should confirm that this incident did not occur. He did apply for the Merchant Navy in 1975 but never heard back from them. He believes this was due to the fact that he included a nude photo with his application to demonstrate his physical prowess.

I will be updating you on how the work progresses. The money should be sent through Western Union. I will be waiting for your mail,

Colin

From: Bob Servant
To: Colin Jackson
Subject: Anything kicking about your studio?

Colin,
Great to hear from you. I'd love to get this painting on the go but I worry that if you paint the thing from scratch then it will take bloody ages. I'm having a 'Pernod and Push-ups Party' in a fortnight and I'd really like the painting for that. Do you have a painting of a man on a boat that we can just pretend is me? Maybe it's in the distance so people would not know? If so, then I could just buy that,

Bob

From: Colin Jackson
To: Bob Servant
Subject: I have one

Hello Bob,
Really do not have the exact painting you are looking for but something close to that, picture below. Let me know what you think. I am happy to sell it but it is a little expensive.[21]

Thanks

From: Bob Servant
To: Colin Jackson
Subject: Bob Looking out to sea

Colin,
That is perfect. I think we could call it 'Bob Looking Out To Sea' and say it shows me looking out from the bridge of Bob's Beauty, looking for icebergs perhaps? What do you think? Does that sound believable to you?

One thing I noticed was that, in the silhouette of my image I am wearing a floppy hat. I don't think that this is what a captain would wear and attach a photo of a more appropriate hat for the final image.

---

21. Here Mr Jackson kindly sent a photo of a contented-looking gentleman looking out with binoculars at a sunset from a ship's bridge. An action, I should say, that I have always been led to believe could lead to instant blindness. Anyway, the photo contains certain identifiable aspects and I have therefore reluctantly removed it.

Your friend,

Bob

From: Colin Jackson
To: Bob Servant
Subject: You must decide

Hey Bob,
It will be a lot of work for me to edit the hat on the already made painting with the one you have sent me, is almost a new job so Bob but I will do. Let me know so we can save time instead of this stress. If you wanted a new painting it would have been almost ready by now! So make up your mind and let me know.

Thanks

Colin

From: Bob Servant
To: Colin Jackson
Subject: Painting

Colin,
Maybe I should go for the existing painting. I could tell people that the reason I was wearing the floppy hat was because it was taken during my break? What do you think? Would you believe that? And, more importantly, would you believe that if you were a woman Colin?

I am desperate to fix something up on the skirt front because Tommy Peanuts recently got together with Daphne Silverstone, the barmaid at Stewpot's Bar. Daphne, I must admit, is a real diamond. She's not as young as she was (she's 68) but my God she still has them hanging over the bar down at Stewpot's. I'm sometimes one of the hangers myself! She does all sorts of shit, leaning over for the peanuts like she doesn't know why we order them, or making saucy comments that send us wild.

Whenever someone orders an apple juice she'll give it – 'Oooh, I feel quite fruity myself', and do that thing where you pretend your eyeballs are rolling backwards into your head. Or if a punter asks if they do sandwiches she'll say, 'Ooooh, are you asking if you can nibble on my buns?' and do the old double-point at her boobs[22] while everyone cheers and bangs their glasses on the bar.

It's all basic, knockabout stuff but with Daphne it just doesn't seem tacky, do you know what I mean? Anyway, Tommy has somehow squired himself up with Daphne and he is ABSOLUTELY BLOODY LOVING IT. Christ, he's walking about the Ferry like he's John Wayne and he keeps pretending to have a bad back just so he can wink and make some rude comment about how he got it.

So the pressure's on old Bob here to come up with something. And I think this painting could be my way in.

Bob

From: Colin Jackson
To: Bob Servant
Subject: Yes I would believe this for sure

Hey Bob,
I think that's exactly what you should tell them, that the picture was taken during a break. Anybody will believe that. Women as well, and this painting will be a big help on you find your own Daphne. Are we now agreed? I can do a special deal but you will have to pay in advance.

Colin

From: Bob Servant
To: Colin Jackson
Subject: YES YOU'RE RIGHT COLIN

Hi Colin,
I think you're right. No-one can see my face or anything like that so as far as they're concerned there's no reason why the figure in the painting shouldn't be me. Even captains have to take breaks sometimes. Also, I

---

22. Stewpot's Bar in Broughty Ferry has never employed a barmaid that behaves in such a manner. 'More's the pity,' said Stewpot when I asked him.

was thinking I could buy a hat like the one in the painting and start wearing it about so if anyone at the party said it wasn't me I could say 'Of course it is, you must have seen me wearing this hat?' and pull it out and they'd have no choice but to agree.

Colin, I would love to see a photo of you at work on a painting or in a studio, is this possible? I'm not being nosey! I just love artists and it would be fantastic to see you at work?

Many thanks,

Bobby

From: Colin Jackson
To: Bob Servant
Subject: Myself in studio

Hello Bob,

How are you doing? I am OK just been a little busy with work. You should know i am a busy man . . . lol.

My pictures at work attached below,[23] then i would really like to make a fresh painting of you in Bob's Beauty? You must finally make up your mind once and for all and tell me what you think i am not always able to check my mail. Looking for your mail. ASAP.

Thanks

Colin

From: Bob Servant
To: Colin Jackson
Subject: Painting Final Order!

Colin,

Great to hear from you and thank you so much for those pictures. I love seeing you working, you look as if you are totally lost in the moment, adrift in the world of art.

I have decided! I want a large painting of the image you have shown me, with 'Bob' (wink wink!) looking out to sea. I would like it framed in a gold frame, or one that looks gold (wink wink!) and underneath I would like the inscription –

'Captain Bob Servant bravely looks out from the bridge of Bob's Beauty. Valentines Day, 1978, somewhere in the Indian Ocean.'

---

23. At this point Mr Jackson supplied several photos of an artist working in a studio. The images have been removed for legal reasons. They're perfectly pleasant shots, they're just very unlikely to feature Mr Jackson.

and then, underneath that, the quotation:

'The Sea Could Not Take Him, No Woman Could Tame Him, No Mountain Too Tall, No River Too Deep, Deep Like His Heart. Bob Servant, Simply The Best. Rocking All Over The World'.

Does that all sound OK? I would like the painting to be done in a gloss finish and to measure 2m long and around 1.5m high as that would look magic above my second sofa. I am very excited by this Colin, very excited indeed.

Bob

PS I had a bit of a debate with Chappy Williams at the Eagle Inn last night Colin. As an artist, do you think in words or pictures? I said I thought you would think in pictures but Chappy said that was a load of shite?

From: Colin Jackson
To: Bob Servant
Subject: OK

Hello Bob,
Thanks again. All the same artist speak both in words and pictures. Remember we have our home, friends, family and social life to live so we speak only in pictures when we are at work Bob! Then about your painting i will do the art work and all the words you want me to print on it sounds OK because it makes you look like a brave captain or rather a hero, lol.

I looking forward to get your mail ASAP and it very important that you send your advance through Western Union so I can get started on Bob's Beauty!

Then the job will be ready within 12 days.

Have a super day,

Colin

From: Bob Servant
To: Colin Jackson
Subject: You have missed the point entirely

Hi Colin,
I did not mean you would speak in pictures, I was asking if you THINK in pictures. If I was to walk up to you in the street and whisper 'mmmm, hello Colin, you look good', then would you think in words 'BOB THINKS I LOOK

GOOD' or would you see YOURSELF as a PICTURE, looking the best that you can? That is what I am interested in. Is it different for you, as an artist?

Bob

From: Colin Jackson
To: Bob Servant
Subject: I now understand Bob

Ok Bob,
I got your mail its alright, I will commence with the Job as soon as you send the advance.

Yes Bob we do think in pictures, I have spent more than 90% of my adulthood in studios painting and thinking of what my customers will appreciate making it as real as possible. When I go shopping with my wife i often stare at things that are around me, imagining them in pictures and dreaming of making paintings of everything I see.

Well hope u are having a nice day. Let me know when you have sent the money Bob.

Colin

From: Bob Servant
To: Colin Jackson
Subject: YOU'RE GOING TO BE IN THE PAPER!

Colin,
I have interesting news! First of all, I have the money ordered and will have it tomorrow. The second is that I was just in the Royal Arch looking for skirt and bumped into Chappy Williams again. Apparently, he has just landed the big one - Broughty Ferry correspondent for the Evening Telegraph.[24] Christ only knows how he got it, he reckons he took a grand off the deputy editor at a poker lock-in at Stewpot's bar and they settled for him getting the gig.[25]

Anyway, I spoke to him about the fact you were doing this painting for me and he was very, very excited. He put down his cocktail (sex on the beach), turned to me and said, 'Fuck me Bob this could be big'. We chatted about it all some more, and he says that he wants to interview you for

---

24. No Chappy Williams has ever been employed by the *Evening Telegraph*, nor has the paper ever had a 'Broughty Ferry correspondent'.
25. The suggestion that the deputy editor of the *Evening Telegraph* would hand out an editorial posting to clear a gambling debt is outrageous and has no basis whatsoever in fact.

the paper! I have had problems with both the local press and my general reputation in the last few years. Or, if I'm being honest, decades. This is an opportunity for me to really bounce back. I told him that you are a busy man so he is only going to send you a few questions. Thanks so much, I will send you the article when it comes out.

Please make me sound like a fun guy when you send Chappy your answers. And, Colin, REMEMBER, two things –

He thinks I was a real captain of Bob's Beauty! Make sure you say that.

Please say that I am very handsome if he asks. That will help me with the skirt and Christ knows I need all the help I can get.

Thank you my friend,

Bob

PS 90% of your life in the studio? That seems a little high?

From: Colin Jackson
To: Bob Servant
Subject: Interview

Hello Captain Bob,

Thanks for your mail and interest in me, but I want to know will the interview be through mail or something? Secondly I will do just like you said {captain in the Bob's Beauty} so you have nothing to worry about because we are in this together.

Then about the money how did you send it? You should send it through Western Union or Moneygram as it will be available for pick-up instantly. You need to send it now, it is very important as we must get this thing started. Let me know when you have done this and Bob's Beauty will kick off.

Have a wonderful day.

Colin

From: Chappy Williams
To: Colin Jackson
Subject: Interview

HELLO COLIN I AM CHAPPY, A FRIEND OF BOB SERVANT AND A TOP NEWSPAPER REPORTER. I HAVE SOME QUESTIONS FOR YOU FOR AN EXCLUSIVE INTERVIEW. PLEASE SEND ME THE ANSWERS AS SOON AS YOU CAN. THANK YOU, CHAPPY.

How long have you been an artist and what was it that made you start?

Bob said that you think in pictures, can you please explain?

How did you meet Bob?

You are doing a painting of Bob in a boat, is it true that he was a captain in the merchant navy? (I have my doubts)

Do you think he is handsome?

What is your favourite thing about Bob?

If you weren't a painter then what do you think you would be?

As a painter, who is your favourite cartoon character? (Mickey Mouse etc)

Thank you very much,

Chappy Williams, Broughty Ferry Correspondent

From: Colin Jackson
To: Bob Servant
Subject: Chappy

Hello Bob,
Your friend Chappy has sent me the questions for the newspaper. Do you want me to answer them in a way that will suit you?

Colin

From: Bob Servant
To: Colin Jackson
Subject: Re: Chappy

Hello Colin,
That's all fine. just send the answers directly to Chappy. Speak to you later. I'm waiting for the woman at the post office to phone me back about this money transfer but she's probably doing her bloody nails or something.

Bob

From: Colin Jackson
To: Chappy Williams
Subject: ANSWERS

Thanks Chappy if you need more information on me you know how to get to me. Tell Bob that I am very grateful for this interview and I am looking forward to read the paper.

Thanks and have a nice day.

Colin

How long have you been an artist and what was it that made you start?

My Dad was an artist and I grow up living with my Dad. It became part of me but I can say that when I officially opened up to the world as a painter was in 1995 when I inherited his studio and became officially know as painter Colin...lol. So I will say that I have been a painter for about 12 years now.

Bob said that you think in pictures can you please explain this?

Well as a painter I actually think in pictures because everything I see around me I imagine them in painting and how they will look if they painted in pictures, so I really imagine a lot of things in paintings especially when I am at work in my studio. I think in pictures as Bob says.

How did you meet Bob?

Well I met Bob on the internet while I was looking for a representative. Bob got my mail and replied asking to see some of my paintings. He grow interest in me and since then I and Bob have been good friends because he is fun talking to and also a caring fellow to know.

You are doing a painting of Bob in a boat, is it true that he was a captain in the Merchant Navy?

Yes I am doing a painting of Bob in Bob's Beauty. For as long as I have been talking to him I know him as Captain Bob because from the day I met him he told me he was a captain in the merchant navy and I believe he is a captain, so if I am asked if Bob is a captain I will say yes.

Do you think he is handsome?

Yes Bob must have been handsome when he was younger because he has worked hard in his jobs to earn a lot of money and so would have got fit along the way. With his good jokes also you can imagine how good he would been with women? I just think the skirts would have been on cue for Bob at his young days! Yes he is a handsome man!

What is your favourite thing about Bob?

My favourite thing about Bob is that he sounds like a good man and I am always pleased to read his mails because he is usually interesting in his writing. Bob must be fun being around.

If you weren't a painter then what do you think you would be?

I would have loved to be an international journalist.

As a painter, who is your favourite cartoon character?

My favourite cartoon is Tom and Jerry and Pink and the Brain.

From: Chappy Williams
To: Colin Jackson
Subject: Thank You

Thanks very much Colin,
I loved the Tom and Jerry joke! The story is all filed and I think it is very funny.

I hope you and Bob enjoy it,

All the best,

Chappy

From: Bob Servant
To: Colin Jackson
Subject: TOM AND FUCKING JERRY?

Colin,
What are you playing at?! Have you seen the Telegraph? What were you thinking? I never said anything about Tom and Jerry, I don't even like the bloody programme.

   I've been getting absolute pelters all day. People keep giving it 'Ooh, Jerry, where's Colin?' And what's all this bollocks about you thinking I'm so handsome? We come across as a right couple of oddballs. By Christ, you've made me look like a complete idiot. Why the hell would I say that we're the new Tom and Jerry. What does that even mean, they were in a fucking cartoon for a start? I wouldn't know where to begin.

I am absolutely furious about this Colin.

Bob

𝔇undee 𝔈vening 𝔗elegraph
𝔅roughty 𝔉erry 𝔑ews   25·02·07

Filed 25.02.07 by Chappy Williams, Broughty Ferry Correspondent

WE'RE LIKE TOM AND JERRY, SAYS PAINTER ABOUT BROUGHTY FERRY MAN

An internationally known artist who has been commissioned by Broughty Ferry resident Bob Servant to produce a portrait has bizarrely claimed that the two of them are the 'new Tom and Jerry'.

Colin Jackson, an English painter who was inspired by his father to pick up the brush back in the 1990s, contacted Servant through the Internet and the two of them hit it off immediately.

'I am always pleased to read Bob's e-mails,' says Jackson, 'because he is usually interesting. Bob must have been a handsome young man, because from the recent pictures he sent me he still looks great, so you can imagine how good he would have been if he was younger?'

It was while e-mailing each other about the painting, which is to show Servant on board a ship called *Bob's Beauty* from his long career in the Merchant Navy, that Jackson claims the two of them decided that they could be the modern-day incarnation of Walt Disney's much loved cartoon duo.

'It was Bob's idea,' says Jackson. 'We both love Tom and Jerry, and he suggested that we could make ourselves like them. He said the world is crying out for a new Tom and Jerry and we would be perfect for the job. I'm not sure how we're going to make ourselves the new Tom and Jerry, because they were cartoon characters but, knowing Bob as I do, he'll have something up his sleeve!'

However, when contacted by the *Evening Telegraph* today, Servant claimed he had no knowledge of the Tom and Jerry plan. 'This is news to me,' he said from Doc Ferry's public bar.[26]

----

26. This article is nowhere to be found in the records of the *Evening Telegraph* for the date given or, indeed, any date in the paper's history. I am very confident in declaring that it was Bob, and not Chappy Williams, who was the author of this piece of fiction.

From: Colin Jackson
To: Bob Servant
Subject: Re: TOM AND FUCKING JERRY?

Hello Bob,
Whats all this about? I only said I liked Tom and Jerry not you so I think your friend Williams should be confronted not me. So i don't see any reason why you should be harassing me like i am some kind of toy or something like that.

Colin

From: Bob Servant
To: Colin Jackson
Subject: I am sorry Colin but this is goodbye

Colin,
I have spoken to Chappy and he is sticking to his story. The last few days have been a complete nightmare and I have been turned into a laughing stock by the Tom and Jerry story. The local radio station had a phone-in yesterday on the matter and the resounding opinion was that I was a basket case.

A taxi driver phoned in from the Seagate rank in Dundee and said that he'd just seen me chasing a mouse down the road with a rubber hammer (which was untrue) and then a woman from Monifieth called and, sounding all pleased with herself, said, "Forget Walt Disney, I think Bob Servant's been on the Malt Whisky."

I knew things were bad when I nipped up to the bowling club and bumped into Jimmy Walker and Bill Wood. Jimmy went to shake my hand and then said, 'Hang on Bob, have you washed your paws?' Then Bill said that the bar was closed so would I be able to nip through the cat flap and get them a couple of drinks? They're both right good guys so when they have a pop you know you're in trouble.

I am sorry Thomas but under the circumstances I cannot take the painting from you. I just want to forget about the whole matter. I do not hold any grudge against you, it's just one of those things. Best of luck for the future,

Yours,

Bob Servant

No Reply

6
Olga, Sasha and the Jamaica Lakers

From: Olga
To: Bob Servant
Subject: From Olga

Hello,
Firstly I want to thank you for reading my email! I want to say I look for someone who is looking for love! My name is Olga Goldovsky. I am 28, a person who loves to joke, attractive, suave and caring. I can be brave and fearless. I live in a wonderful part of our Earth named Chelyabinsk, in ural Mountains. My parents died when I was 10 in car crash and my grandma brought me up. What else... My favourite color is white, color of innocence. My favourite flowers are white lilies and I wish that on my wedding day. In the end I want to say I sincerely want to know you better and hope you want the same.

Best wishes, Olga.

From: Bob Servant
To: Olga
Subject: Howdy

Olga,
What a welcome surprise. Tell me - are you athletic? Do you have any statistics (just basic stuff - 100m, hurdles, javelin) that you could offer in evidence? This is very important,

Your Servant,

Bob Servant

From: Olga
To: Bob Servant
Subject: From Olga

How are you dear Bob?
I am fine and very glad you answered. It is a real pleasure to receive your letter. I get the feeling we will hit off. This is the first attempt by me to use this medium to find a soul mate, and it is certainly the last because I find a "gold mine" whose other name is yours (smile). I will have no other man in my life except you. I want to know your mysteries and desires. I'm sincere with you and I'd like to devote my life to you, to give you my soul and body.

With kisses,

Olga

From: Bob Servant
To: Olga
Subject: Wotcha

Olga,
You are a wonderful woman, with a great smile and a winning personality but we have a problem. In the previous email I asked you a question you did not answer. If you want to be my wife then it is vital that you listen to me otherwise the whole house of cards will collapse directly into our eyeballs.

Bob

From: Olga
To: Bob Servant
Subject: From Olga

My dear Bob,
Dear telling the truth I didn't understand exactly your question but if it is about sport I want to say that I am not fond of sport. But you have made my day a lot better after knowing that you are attracted to me and that you would like to get to know me. I dream often about having my own house but it is very expensive to do so. In the end of my letter it is true to say that I am looking for full commitment, friendship and romance from you.

With tender thoughts,

Olga

From: Bob Servant
To: Olga
Subject: Your homeowning dream

Olga,

Sorry to hear about your problems getting on the property ladder. I took the liberty of investigating this for you and have found this article. www.regnum.ru/english/1059675.html

As you will see, Vladimir Dyatlov (the deputy governor in charge for economy, construction and infrastructure of Chelyabinsk Region, as if I need to tell you) is making some very positive noises about local housing costs.[27]

I think if you sit tight, things will definitely loosen up as part of the credit crunch. Prices are fairly tumbling here. Nervous Norrie reckons his caravan is losing twenty pounds a week.

Bob

From: Olga
To: Bob Servant
Subject: From Olga

Hello darling Bob!

Thank you once again for writing back to me, I so enjoy receiving your letters. The economy has not let me buy a house even with these troubles but let us not talk too much about houses because I am so happy that our attraction to one another is mutual. My feelings for you seem to be growing more and more with each passing day! I look forward to what the future will bring! You are the man I have been searching for my whole life. I am so excited about building a life together with you,

Olga.

----

27. This article does indeed strongly indicate a weakening housing market in the troubled Chelyabinsk region.

From: Bob Servant
To: Olga
Subject: Don't give up that easily.

Olga,
I'll be honest, I'm surprised at just how forcefully you are throwing yourself
into this relationship but you're such a cracking piece of skirt that you won't
be getting any arguments from old Bobby Boy. I think you are giving up a
little easily on the housing issue. Perhaps you should alert the local paper.
It looks like the biggest paper in Chelyabinsk is Vyecherny Chelyabinsk. I
strongly suggest you contact them and volunteer to write a dramatic first
person account of your problems –

"My housing heartache by Olga Goldovsky".

Or the more lighthearted –

"Knock Knock. Who's there? Olga Goldovsky and I'd Like to Buy a House
But I Can't".

Please send me a link to the article when it's published. I'll see if the
Broughty Ferry Gazette will carry a Scottish version. Christ only knows
who'll translate it. There's a few Polish boys putting a new roof on the
chemists in Queen Street, I could ask them?

Bob

PS Nice couch.

From: Olga
To: Bob Servant
Subject: From "Lotos"

Dear Sir,
We inform you that Olga is our client. She uses our Internet and
translation services but unfortunately she cannot reply to your last letter
due to lack of funds. She wants you know that she is very interested in
you and further correspondence. If you wish to continue your intercourse
with Olga we can send you the information about our services and prices
in order to proceed.

Respectfully,
Principal of "Lotos"
Sasha Malikov

From: Bob Servant
To: Olga
Subject: Hi Sasha

Sasha,

Thanks for getting in touch and pass on my best wishes to Olga. I must say, it's very decent of her to let you use her email address. Sasha, I would like you to help me. Man to man. Olga is top drawer but is she as good as she seems? She says she loves me, which is obviously fantastic news, but I just worry that she's getting too carried away. Please can you help me with these questions –

1.) Olga seems to be both obsessed and also clearly frightened by houses. Did a house once do something bad to her? Maybe she was electrocuted by a door bell or got her hand trapped in a letter box?

2.) Is Olga as beautiful as she looks in the photos?

3.) Is she honest?

4.) How large are her hands? (It is hard to see in the photos)

Many thanks,

Bob Servant

From: Olga
To: Bob Servant
Subject: From "Lotos"

Dear Sir,

Thanks. I can see Olga's sincere interest in you and her willingness to communicate with you. Olga tells me she does not care for houses this was misunderstanding on your part. Olga is indeed very beautiful as you will have seen and she is really an honest girl and truly wants to find her second half. As for your other question Olga has hands as beautiful as herself. So if you are interested in her let us know.

Respectfully,

"Lotos".

From: Bob Servant
To: Olga
Subject: Do I look cool in the pool?

Sasha,

You have really put my mind at rest, especially with regards to her hands. This is extremely important because my ex-wife had hands like shovels and it drove me round the fucking bend. They'd flap about like no-one's business and were always getting trapped in things and becoming all red and cut up. If she ruffled my hair it was like I was being attacked by a monster and when she got to grips with the old boy it was like being pleasured by a fairground worker.

I am now 98% sure that Olga is honest and just trying to make her way through the jungle. As, of course, am I. I have attached a photo. It shows me lounging in my swimming pool in Broughty Ferry. What do you think? If I look ugly then DO NOT UNDER ANY CIRCUMSTANCES show it to Olga. If I look spunky then pass it on. By Christ I hope she likes it. Tell her that they're only my third best pair of trunks. And say that my belly is sticking out because of the way I'm lying. And tell her that I've been doing a lot of weightlifting since then.

Yours,

Bob

From: Olga
To: Bob Servant
Subject: From "Lotos"

Dear Sir,
I can see you are honest and truthful and sincerely interested in Olga. As for your photos, my opinion is you look very attractive. I think that Olga would be glad. She is impatiently waiting for your communication. The services we provide are

one month of unlimited correspondence - 200 USD;
two months of unlimited correspondence - 350 USD;
three months of unlimited correspondence - 500 uSD.

We also provide unlimited translation, printing photos for your lady and scanning your lady's photos. You make payment via Western union. When your account is filled you can write to your lady and get responses.

Respectfully,
Principal of "Lotos",
Sasha Malikov.

From: Bob Servant
To: Olga
Subject: Great News

Sasha,
I'm getting excited. Olga is an absolute gem, isn't she? A real Russian Revelation. A Moscow Majesty. Putin's Peach! Thanks for talking me through your packages. I would love to keep my communication with Olga ticking over. I hope we can talk more and maybe even discuss her coming to live with me in Scotland. But please do not tell her that bit yet, I want to surprise her. There is one more thing however, that I have to ask you. I need to show you something but I need you to promise not to show Olga.

Do you promise?

Bob

From: Olga
To: Bob Servant
Subject: From "Lotos"

Dear Sir,
Don't be offended but we have a lot of clients at the firm and I can't pay enough attention for your letters and my answers. Moreover Olga comes

to the firm every day and asks whether you write. If you wish to continue your correspondence you should pay our fees.

Respectfully,
Sasha Malikov,
"Lotos".

From: Bob Servant
To: Olga
Subject: Treat me with Respect

Sasha,

I have to say I'm a little angry with you. Of course I want to continue my communication with Olga, I have already said that I may be falling in love with the bloody woman. But first I needed to ask you some questions, Mano-a-Mano, to help me decide if she is the one.

You are acting as if you are worried I will not pay. Sasha, do I really have to remind you about Dundee's Cheese Burger Wars of 1988-89? You must remember the coverage, it was on North Tonight every day for a month. Well, remember the spokesman for the Cheese Burger Van Owners (CHEBUVAO) that was on most nights? The dashing man in the bunnet, sometimes just credited as 'Cheese Burger Tycoon'? He said things like –

"The public want cheeseburgers and I am giving them cheeseburgers,"

"I'm making money but I'm also making happiness. And that's the important thing, as well as the money,"

and, "The council are fannies"?

Well Sasha, that was me. You might also have caught the North Tonight Special Report with that stitch-up of a debate.[28] They beam North Tonight out to the boys on the rigs so it might have made it to Russia. Anyway, the end result of those years was me sitting on more cash than you would believe. Fair enough, the boo boys would say that I blew some of it. The

---

28. On 8 August 1988 Bob Servant appeared on Grampian Television's North Tonight Special Report entitled 'Cheese Burger or Cheese Murder?' The other guests were a local councillor and a member of the Scottish Obesity Forum. The debate lasted just short of three minutes during which time Bob accused the Scottish Obesity Forum of being both Communists and 'perverts', accused the councillor of being 'knee deep in bungs from the kebab shops' and then angrily suggested that the show's presenter (who had yet to speak) was 'putting words in my mouth'. Bob walked off the set, only to reappear twenty seconds later to ask who he should speak to about expenses, at which point the show was replaced without warning by an old edition of Sheepdog Trials.

Topless Dentists idea cost me a small fortune, I'm man enough to admit that.

But don't forget the windowcleaning. In the early 90s I had the largest window cleaning round in Western Europe. Maybe you had something better behind the Iron Curtain, and if so I hold my hands up, but what I'm saying Sasha is give me the respect that my achievements deserve. I attach a photo of my wallet.

Bob

From: Olga
To: Bob Servant
Subject: From "Lotos"

Dear Bob,

I didn't want to offend you I just wanted to explain my situation. I might have seen this TV programme. Of course you can share your thoughts with me. I understand your feelings that you want to take the right decision concerning Olga. So I want to let you know that you can ask me any question you want and it will stay confidential. I promise.

Sasha Malikov.

From: Bob Servant
To: Olga
Subject: Apology Accepted

Sasha,

OK, I am just going to tell you. I BEG YOU not to tell Olga until we've worked out the best way forward. Sasha, I am a man without a sword. I have no thingy. It all happened two years ago. I'd been up all night, drinking in the garden (it was the summer) and trying to build a tree house with my old rabbit hutch. Frank Theplank was there for a bit but I told him to leave because all he brought to the party was two cans of Kestrel and a Curly Wurly.

Come morning I was fairly gone, shouting army stuff and running round the place dressed only in my vest. I made an assault course using my Superman duvet (tunnelling net), Christmas tree lights (limbo challenge), all my forks (pit made by Cannibals that I had to jump over) and tennis balls - I would throw them at the wall and had to dodge them when they bounced off. I called that Alien Attack but it wasn't really that good.

I decided that the front gate should be the winning post for the assault course and after a few attempts was sitting at 2 minutes and 5 seconds as my record. I decided that I could take things up a gear. Sasha, the number of times that I wish that I had not made that decision - that my stupid pride had let me sit tight at 2 minutes, 5 seconds. No-one was going to beat that.

But I went for it. I flew under that duvet like a man possessed, nearly broke my bloody spine on the limbo, cleared the Cannibal's forks by a yard and the Aliens didn't even get close with their laser tennis balls. Then I set off for the front gate. I felt like I was in Chariots of Fire with the wind running through my hair and over my innocently exposed genitals.

I got through the gate with my arms raised skywards but as I did so I stumbled on the step. As I fell that I saw the paperboy speeding along the pavement on his bike. He swerved as I fell sideways into him and I'll never forget our eyes locking just for a moment as my old boy - poor little Bobby Junior, swung into his rotating spokes.

The pain, Sasha, was like nothing I could describe. A milkman told me a few months later they had heard my scream from the Forthill Dairy, half a mile away. But what's worse is how it left me. A soldier without a gun. A shepherd without a dog. A cowboy without a horse.[29] Oh, Sasha. Whatever will Olga think? I would attach a photo, but I don't want to put you off your lunch.

Yours in hope,

Bob "No Nob" Servant

From: Olga
To: Bob Servant
Subject: From "Lotos"

Dear Bob,
I read your letter. I promise that I won't tell Olga and it will stay between us. As a man I understand what a great trouble this truly is. There is no problem without answer and there are some modern methods to help. Moreover I think Olga is more interested in your inner world.

---

29. I can personally verify, due to the confines of the men's lavatory in Doc Ferry's bar and Bob's peculiar sense of humour, that Bob has not suffered this particular loss.

I think true and sincere love will overcome all obstacles and you shouldn't worry. Olga is a very kind, understanding and caring person and she is able to understand you. But I promise not to tell Olga, it is your right to tell her. I will help you with my advice or anything else you need. Are you ready to open your account?

Sincerely,

Sasha Malikov.

From: Bob Servant
To: Olga
Subject: Do you think I should buy one of these three?

Sasha,

Thank you Sasha, from the bottom of my (Tony) heart, for those words that make me feel like crying hot tears of gratitude. I can't tell you how difficult it's been since I lost Bobby Junior in the paperboy's bike. I cannot consider surgery at my age so I've been thinking about some sort of artificial replacement.

I have attached photos of three possibilities. Let me know your thoughts. The first one looks like a serious bit of kit and it clearly wouldn't fit down my pants. I'd have to carry it in the pocket of a long jacket or maybe a shopping bag. But you can't exactly go carrying about a shopping bag with a mechanical cock in it can you? Certainly not anywhere there might be children, or down at the swimming baths.

The second would work well stuffed down my pants but I'd have to warm it up first. The third is interesting. It looks useful in the bedroom and also good fun to play with. I am waiting for your thoughts. I find it hard to talk to other men about this because they'd take the piss. If the boys down at Stewpot's got hold of this I'd be finished. I hope Olga is well, I have been thinking about her and looking at those wonderful photographs. The ones of her that is, not the photos of the false cocks.

Yours Respectfully,

Bob

From: Olga
To: Bob Servant
Subject: From "Lotos"

Bob,

I thought a lot about your problem and these artificial options. Unfortunately I can't advise you anything. You should discuss all this with Olga as it will affect her directly. Please look to create funds in your account as this is something you must discuss with her soon.

Respectfully,

"Lotos".

From: Bob Servant
To: Olga
Subject: Let's test her Sasha....

Sasha,

I've an idea. Could you speak to Olga and pretend to tell her about a friend of yours who does not have an old boy because of an accident he was in? Of course, you're talking about me, but this way we can test her reaction. Just say it's a Russian friend, maybe call him Boris or something?

If you start, "Olga, did I ever tell you about my friend Boris? The funniest thing happened to him....", and then take it from there.

Be very laidback and HOPEFULLY she will be chilled out about it also. If she reacts as if this would be a problem and she, as a woman, would want nothing to do with Boris then we will have hit a brick wall. However, it would be best to find out as I'm sure you wouldn't want me to waste my money otherwise. Praying for a positive reaction,

Bob

From: Olga
To: Bob Servant
Subject: From "Lotos"

Bob,

I have some news. Olga came asking about you. It was an opportunity to talk. I chose my words carefully and told her about a friend with such problem. I told it so it was not about you. She listened very attentively. After finishing my story she said that she has a girlfriend who's boyfriend has the same problems.

Olga told me her girlfriend loves her boyfriend and it doesn't matter whether he has "the thing" or not. Olga also told her attitude. She said the main thing in relations is mutual understanding and love. If a couple has this nothing else matters and they overcome everything. She will confirm this I am sure when you place funds in your account.

Sasha.

From: Bob Servant
To: Olga
Subject: Great Stuff

That is really good news. Is there any way you could get me the email address of the Russian guy who also lost his pecker? I'd love to swap war stories and hopes for the future.

From: Olga
To: Bob Servant
Subject: From "Lotos"

Bob,
No I cannot that would not be fair. Bob, I cannot talk to you any more if you do not choose a package and send funds. It is not fair on the other customers. Send money today even $50 to get started. You deserve it with everything that has happened to you. But do not hesitate too long as you must remember a woman has many admirers. There is an English man who wants to take Olga on vacation already.

Sasha.

From: Bob Servant
To: Olga
Subject: English thief

You what?! Where's he taking her? The cheeky bastard. You'd better warn him off Sasha I'm serious. I know people down there. Chappy has a cousin in Birmingham who knows ju-jitsu.

From: Olga
To: Bob Servant
Subject: From "Lotos"

He is talking about taking her to Jamaica. If you are quick and pay money into your account I can talk her into staying and coming to your country if you add money enough for air fare.

Sasha

From: Bob Servant
To: Olga
Subject: TELL HER TO STAY RIGHT THERE

Sasha,
Do you both have valid passports? I have a plan. Tell the English boy to sling his hook.

Bob

From: Olga
To: Bob Servant
Subject: From Sasha

Bob,
How are you? Olga asked about you. As for the passports, yes we have them. Olga asked if you send air fare for her to come and visit. Otherwise I do not know how much I can do to stop her going on vacation with this English client. Why do you ask about passports? Can you send even $50 to open your account?

Sasha.

From: Bob Servant
To: Olga
Subject: OK, here is my plan

Sasha,
This is going to knock your socks off. I want you AND Olga to come to Scotland. I really, really like you Sasha and I think the three of us make a good team. Once you're both here, this is what we're going to do. We are going to form a business called

BIG BOBBY BOY AND THE JAMAICA LAKERS.

There's two main reasons for this Sasha. The first is that I can't get this English bigshot out my head. I'm not a jealous man but I don't want Olga to arrive in Broughty Ferry and have just a tiny bit of her saying, '"Fuck me, I wish I was in Jamaica". So I'm going to bring Jamaica to her. Secondly, we're going to have to keep ourselves busy or we'll start to annoy each other and I know you and Olga are two people who would always want to work for a living and aren't interested in handouts.

Let me tell you about the business. There's some people in Broughty Ferry with big houses and gardens and I think a lot of them would be interested in having a small Jamaica Lake installed. What's a Jamaica Lake? I'll tell you. A Jamaica Lake Sasha, is fun. That's all, just fun.

I'm sure you and Olga will have your own views on what the lakes should look like. My initial thoughts are that we could shape them like a big thumbs up and/or have rocks that are actually speakers and played Chaka Demus and the Pliers whenever anyone comes within ten yards and says 'Jamaica?' in a clear voice. If you didn't have that voice code in place then the music would be set off by the postie in the morning and cats and foxes at night.

My other idea was that we could make dreadlocks out of twisted up bin bags and stretch them across the water so the lake has hair like the boys in Jamaica. We would have to put a small sign up saying that this was not real hair or someone passing by might think that a Rasta was drowning and dive into the lake. The lakes would only be about a foot deep so any rescue attempt could lead to paralysis.

What do you think? This is how I see BIG BOBBY AND THE JAMAICA LAKERS breaking down -

BOB SERVANT - Chief Architect, Head of Sales, Accountant.

SASHA MALIKOV - Head of Digging, Chief Translator (for Olga and any Russian clients)

OLGA GOLDOVSKY - Head of Foliage, Sandwich Maker

Sasha, I think we would be a big success. I know I'm asking a lot. You've worked like a soldier to build up Lotos from scratch but I think this could be an opportunity for you to get away from the madness of the Lotos office and the Russian Ratrace and work in the open air.

What do you say?

From: Olga
To: Bob Servant
Subject: From Sasha

Bob,

Olga and I have considered this and decided that yes we will both come to your country and work in this new area. The airfare for Olga is $1400. I will pay my own air fare but to close my business here is a fine of $2000. This is $3400 that it is fair enough for you to pay. Can you send by Western union? Can you send today and then Olga and I can plan our trip.

From: Bob Servant
To: Olga
Subject: Ticket

Sasha,
Great news. I'll book Olga's flight directly, that would be easiest. What's her passport number?

From: Olga
To: Bob Servant
Subject: From Sasha

Bob,
If you send me the money then we will book Olga's flight here. This is what she would rather do. Can you send the $3400 today by Western Union?

From: Bob Servant
To: Olga
Subject: Ticket

What difference does it make if I just book it?

From: Olga
To: Bob Servant
Subject: From Sasha

Bob,
Olga says she would rather book it from here. She is a proud woman like you know and would want to book it herself. I am also proud Russian man and so I must pay this fine to my partners for leaving Lotos. Are you sending the money today?

Sasha

From: Bob Servant
To: Olga
Subject: My mistake

Sasha,
Of course. I forgot how proud you both are. You have demonstrated that to me in many ways, particularly by agreeing to fly to Scotland to join a new company making Jamaica lakes. Sasha, one thing I forgot to say. When

the two of you come here, then Olga will obviously stay in the house with me but I think it would be awkward with you around as well.

Would you mind, and I know this sounds a bit daft, living in a dustbin? I have a spare dustbin that I haven't used for years. It's quite big and relatively comfortable, as dustbins go. You can still use the kitchen and the bathroom in the house but after we have our dinner and all watch a bit of telly it would be a case of Olga and I going to bed and you going outside and getting into the dustbin. Is that OK with you?

From: Olga
To: Bob Servant
Subject: From Sasha

Bob,

I am OK whatever the arrangement. It is cold here in Russia so living outside will not be a problem. Bob, please, you must send the money immediately. Olga is now thinking that maybe you are not serious. I know you are but it is hard to keep her OK. Send the money today, you understand? $3400.

Sasha

From: Bob Servant
To: Olga
Subject: Last Request

One last thing. As you know, I am not in possession of a you-know-what and I really miss the old boy. I miss the stuff with skirt but also something else. One of the great pleasures of my life, Sasha, was standing above the toilet, holding Bobby Junior and unleashing for as long as I possibly could. I always tried to keep the flow as slow as possible. I never pushed myself, I let things happen naturally and kept an eye on my watch to see how I was doing. On a blackboard beside the toilet I had BOBBY JUNIOR'S TOP TEN where I kept my longest times.

In 1996, after hosting a cider war between myself, Tommy Peanuts and Frank Theplank I stopped myself going to the toilet until I couldn't walk standing up. When I finally went, Sasha, I hit one minute, eight seconds.

Now, that time will never be beaten but you've got no idea how many nights I wish I could have another crack at it. Going to the toilet these days, as you can imagine, is no fun and that's where you come in.

I was thinking Sasha, and of course you'd have to be comfortable with this, that I could come with you to the toilet. You would stand at the toilet and I would hold your old boy as you went. This would not in any way be a saucy set-up. I would wear a glove, probably a goalie's glove to maintain a good grip and I would also look straight ahead. Other than that, you could just go as normal and we'd see how we did time wise. Obviously, I'd give you great support, saying things like –

"Easy, Sasha, easy, don't force it".

"Give me a little bit more big guy, just a little bit more".

And – "Waterfalls Sasha, waterfalls".

What do you think? I wouldn't be angry if you didn't do well time wise, I'd just be glad to be back in the hunt. Look forward to hearing your thoughts,

Bob Servant

From: Olga
To: Bob Servant
Subject: From Sasha

OK Bob,
I have thought about this and it sounds OK as well. YOU MUST SEND $3400 THROUGH WESTERN UNION. Can you do this today Bob? Olga is worried and a little angry.

Sasha

From Bob Servant
To: Olga
Subject: I give up

(No message)

From: Olga
To: Bob Servant
Subject: From Sasha

Bob,
What do you mean?

Sasha

NO REPLY/THE END

7
The Hunt For Jerren Jimjams

From: Dr. Mamadou Kouassi
To: Bob Servant
Subject: Opportunity

Dearest,
TRANSFER OF US$25m INTO A PERSONAL/COMPANY'S
OFFSHORE ACCOUNT

We solicit your assistance. We have US$25m made from over inflated
contracts in my Ministry (Federal Ministry of Education) here in
Senegal. We seek your assistance to remit this amount into your account
or any nominated account. Your commission will be 20% of the total
sum, 10% for expenses and the remaining 70% for my colleagues
and myself. Could you notify me of your acceptance to carry out this
transaction along with your private Tel. And Fax number.

Yours faithfully,

Dr. Mamadou Kouassi

From: Bob Servant
To: Dr. Mamadou Kouassi
Subject: Opportunity

I cannot help you. I simply do not trust anyone from Senegal because
the name of the country is so close to seagull. I am sure you get this all
the time, and I know it's not your fault, but I hope you can understand my
reasons,

Bob

From: Dr. Mamadou Kouassi
To: Bob Servant
Subject: From Dr. M Kouassi

Dear Mr Bob Servant,
I receive your mail with thanks. Has maybe a Senegal man done you
wrong before and that is the reason why you do not want this? I am
not blaming you. Forward the hooligans name and contact information
so that i can make an entry, yes i have the power. I forward to police
headquarters to trace them and catch them red-handed. Whatever you lost
you are going to gain it. Concerning my offer i don't know your opinion.
Do you have details for a personal/company or offshore account?

THANK YOU AND AWAITING YOUR REPLY.

Dr. Mamadou

From: Bob Servant
To: Dr Mamadou Kouassi
Subject: You got it

Marmalade,
That's right, you've understood me perfectly. The seagull was a red herring. The man from Senegal who ripped me off called himself –

JERREN JIMJAMS

Frankly I'm not sure if that is his real name. He said he had this secret bank account with $25m, I'd get 25%, and so on. The usual bollocks you get from that lot. I paid him over $50,000 and I never heard from him again. JERREN JIMJAMS is a liar and a fraud and I hate him,

Bob

PS Sorry I don't want to do the new deal after my experiences. I also don't have an offshore bank account. Chappy Williams has a cousin that works on the oil rigs so he may have one, I'll check for you. They have a great time the rig boys, they pay fuck-all tax and spend their time fishing and sunbathing.[30]

From: Dr. Mamadou Kouassi
To: Bob Servant
Subject: Dr. M. Kouassi

Dear Mr Bob Servant,
Please my friend my name is Mamadou. I thank you for the information of the money. Believe me we will locate JERREN JIMJAMS since Dakar is a small place. The only thing you will do now is to send to me his phone and fax number so the operation begins at police headquarter. You give me the bank you were using at the time. I guarantee you we recover your money. They will vomit the money by force.

Thank you and remain bless.

Dr. Mamadou Kouassi.

---

30. Bob is presumably referring to the nearby North Sea oilfields. Employees of the oil companies pay national rates of taxation. The suggestion that they spend time fishing and sunbathing, on one hundred metre high oil rigs stationed halfway to Norway, is frankly ridiculous.

From: Bob Servant
To: Dr Mamadou Kouassi
Subject: Vomit

Marmalade,
It would be great to see them vomit the money. Let me check my files for JIMJAMS phone number. He called from a mobile. There was load music playing and I could hear a woman laughing. She had a strange laugh. It kind of stopped and then started then stopped and then REALLY started and no-one else was laughing so I think she was either reading something funny in the newspaper or maybe watching You've Been Framed but only she could see the television? Also I remember JIMJAMS said he lived beside the sea and had long hair. That at least gives you something to go on in the meantime. Maybe I should speak to the police directly?

Bob

From: Dr. Mamadou Kouassi
To: Bob Servant
Subject: THE GENDARMERIE

Dear Mr Bob Servant,
It is Mamadou that you call me. These are useful tips. Now I have already laid the complaint and the Gendarmerie police assure me as long as you provide the contact of the criminal that he will be caught within days. As you describe JIMJAMS lives near sea and has long hair the order has been given to round up those who have this description. He said that you should contact him

Email: Gendarmerie_office@yahoo.fr

Name: YOUSSOU BA (GENDARMERIE)

Please my friend i advice you send him an email and explain everything to him. Rest assured this GENDARMERIE is an action man.

Dr Mamadou Kouassi.

From: Bob Servant
To- Youssou Ba
Subject: For the Urgent Attention of Mr Youssou Ba

Dear Sir,
A good friend of mine, who I shall not name for the purpose of keeping him safe from the rebels, told me you can help me trap the notorious JERREN JIMJAMS who took me for over $50,000. I know that he has long hair

and a female associate with a distinctive laugh. I would warn your men that JIMJAMS is a cruel and cunning thief. A man like him does not need weapons. His weapon is his mouth. Please beware. JIMJAMS might try and talk your men into letting him go. He will mess with their minds and undress them with his eyes. He is a coyote, a real snake in the grass. I have attached a photo which I think he may look a little bit like,

Thank you,

Bob

From: Youssou Ba
To: Bob Servant
Subject: GENDARMERIE in charge

Atten: Mr Bob,
Well I recieved your mail with thanks and am obliged to see the photo of the so-called JERREN JIMJAMS. Now I have printed the photo and dispatched it to the whole offices for proper investigation. You should not worry on how my boys apprehend him. In my country the people living near the sea is not populated and I will send my boys to the zone tomorrow. Everybody will present their ID and passport and anybody with the name JERREN JIMJAMS will suffer hell.

I will like to inform you that you will pay me £5,000 when i get him but you have to bear in mind that you will come down as soon as i get the robber so that we can recover all your money. You will pay me 1/2 the money immediately when I catch them and bring the rest with you.

I will like you to send to me your phone and fax number including your residential address.

MR YOUSSOU BA

GENDARMERIE INCHARGE.

From: Bob Servant
To: Youssou Ba
Subject: Progress

Youssou,

Your tactics for trapping JIMJAMS are spot on with one flaw. I am talking, of course, about the sea. Let's not leave the back door open. The land assault should be complemented by a simultaneous naval attack. All ports should be blocked off and any ship that tries to break through should get one shot across the bows and then just blow those fuckers right out of the water Youssou. It's up to you if you lead the land or naval charge. I would base the decision on whether you get seasick and what outfit you look best in.

I will happily pay a £5,000 reward when JIMJAMS is caught, with one demand. When you catch him I want you (personally) to strip him naked and dress him in women's clothes. This is an old British tradition. It is a way of humiliating criminals and making them look like dafties. For example, here is a photo of a man recently caught stealing bread in Monifieth,[31]

Speak soon, best of luck,

Bob

----

31. Monifieth's bread thieves, or thieves of any nature, are not required to dress in such a manner following capture. Doing so would likely be seen as a cheap attempt at claiming diminished responsibility.

From: Youssou Ba
To: Bob Servant
Subject: Send your phone and fax urgently

Attn: Bob Servant ,
I inform you that 9 men were apprehended and are waiting for
interrogation. Send me your phone and fax immediately and prepare to
send money through Western Union and also to come here to Dakar to
collect the rest of your money.

Sincerely,

Mr Youssou Ba.

From: Bob Servant
To: Youssou Ba
Subject: Easy on the interrogation

Great news. Take it easy with the questioning. Get inside their heads
Youssou, see what makes them tick. Where is the best place to fly to? I will
have to really shake up my travelling wardrobe for this one. I am going to
set the reward for the capture of JIMJAMS at £5,000. You can use this any
way you see fit - ie, bribes, gifts, or the setting up of honey traps. Any word
from Dr Kouassi? I miss him a bit but not too much because you sound so
like him.

Yours,

Bob x

From: Youssou Ba
To: Bob Servant
Subject: Jimjams apprehended

Attn: Mr Bob Servant,
Dr Kouassi is just OK and happy because I have updated him with this.
After the 9 men were treated like goats they confessed the truth. We
found JIMJAMS office where he used to set all his boys and the second
boss of JIMJAMS told us where his mansion was. JIMJAMS was
arrested at his mansion at 5am. He is in jail. He has agreed he took your
money and that he took an American man's money as well. JIMJAMS has
long hair and criminal eyes you were right about this. Now I want you to
prepare yourself to come to Dakar and send £2,500 as we agree.

Mr Youssou Ba.

GENDARMERIE

From: Bob Servant
To: Youssou Ba
Subject: Incredible Scenes

Youssou,
You have him? JIMJAMS is captured? Thank Christ. Youssou, all I ask is
this. Make JIMJAMS dress in women's clothes and take a photo. I need to
see that photo and then I will know that he is captured and humiliated. I will
send £5,000 reward when I know this is the case,

Bob

From: Youssou Ba
To: Bob Servant
Subject: Awaiting Urgently

Attn: Mr Bob Servant,
My dear here is the photo of Jimjams in the woman's clothes. Now I need
the money to settle my boys. You can send it by Western Union to these
details.

MR YOUSSOU BA
SENEGAL - DAKAR
WEST AFRICA

From: Bob Servant
To: Youssou Ba
Subject: Oops!

Youssou,
My friend, surely that is just the photo that I sent you with some black stuff clumsily added to the shot, presumably to look like some sort of shawl? I think you've clicked on the wrong file. I can't wait to see the proper photo of JIMJAMS in women's clothing.

All the very best,

Bob

From: Youssou Ba
To: Bob Servant
Subject: Send money now

Dear Mr Bob Servant,
In fact it is a shameful thing that you are not trusting your friends that are fighting for you. Bob, forget about the photo. My bosses has ordered that nobody is allowed to see JIMJAMS until further notice. Please give me your flight schedule and send the money agreed for now today please.

Thank you.

Mr Youssou Ba.

GENDARMERIE

From: Bob Servant
To: Youssou Ba
Subject: Photo, Dinner rules

Youssou,
No problem. Just tell your bosses that I give permission. Tell them Bob wants the skirt shot or the gig's up. That should do the trick. I am planning to travel at the end of the week and would like to take this opportunity to invite you and your team out to dinner. I will pay for this over and above the agreed £5,000. You can have starters and main course OR main course and dessert. I will also buy a bottle of wine for every two people. Please let me know your thoughts on what courses the men would like.

Bob

From: Youssou Ba
To: Bob Servant
Subject: Assure me that you are coming

Attn: Mr Bob Servant,

I just received your mail now and I was wondering the type of insult
that you are giving me? I used my power to have the so-called Jimjams
arrested and detained just for your sake to recover your money. My dear
the law of this country prohibits me to call a photographer to picture
Jimjams in the cell, but you are telling me to picture him before you
come and collect your money. If you want you can sleep in the cell with
Jimjams if that is your cup of tea.

My friend I will only detain this man for a few days until you send the
£2,500. The American man has already paid and it looks he will get back
every penny stolen from him by JIMJAMS.

We will have starters and then the main meal.

Thank you.

Mr Youssou Ba.

GENDARMERIE

From: Bob Servant
To: Youssou Ba
Subject: An American you say?

Youssou,

There's a Yank involved in this vipers nest? That reassures me greatly
and I am willing to abandon the photo request. Could I please have this
American's email address?

My flight is waiting to be confirmed. Many thanks for your offer to share
a cell with JIMJAMS. However, I do not think this would be practical on a
security level and I will stay in a hotel. You can stay with me if you like?

Bob

From: Youssou Ba
To: Bob Servant
Subject: Assure me that you are coming

Attn: Mr Bob Servant,

Thank you for your mail and is well noted. Regarding the America man
that Jimjams betrayed for $72,000USD.

Name : Randy Whyting
Email: gorWhyting@ ███████████

Thanks and awaiting for your arrival?

Mr Youssou Ba

Gendarmerie

From: Bob Servant
To: Randy Whyting
Subject: For the Attention of Mr. Randy Whyting

Randy,

How are you? You don't know me but I am a British cheeseburger van operator (retired) and windowcleaner (resting) and gigolo (unemployed, through choice)[32] named Bob Servant. We have a common purpose - JERREN JIMJAMS. I am sure that just saying that name has sent a shiver down your American neck under your cowboy hat. Please, tell me what happened in your case?

   In mine, JIMJAMS pretended to have access to millions of dollars. When I paid him over $50,000 the guy legged it. Luckily I met a wonderful couple of chaps, a doctor and a policeman from Senegal. I'm not sure what's happened to the doctor but the policeman has managed to nab JIMJAMS after a large-scale land and sea assault. I think he's a great guy. Whereabouts in America are you?

Your Servant,

Bob Servant

---

32. The 'Services Offered' column of the *Broughty Ferry Gazette* contained an advertisement every Saturday for the first few months of 2008 entitled 'Cuddles and Maybe More?' 'Calling all Lonely Skirt' the advert declared, 'A local late 50s/early 60s gigolo is now available. Strong arms, spotless bunnet, beautiful singing voice. Treat yourself. Rates Negotiable'. An advertisement on Saturday April 23rd announced: 'Gigolo no Longer Available'. 'Local late 50s/early 60s gigolo is no longer available' it reads. 'This is NOT due to lack of interest. I am leaving with my head held high. Whoever I am'. An advertisement on Saturday April 30th is titled 'To Gigolo Bob, Thanks Anyway'. 'Happy retirement wishes to the local unused gigolo Bob Servant of Harbour View Road', it reads. 'All the best from the boys at Stewpot's Bar'. The advertisement is then signed by eighteen men.

From: Randy Whyting
To: Bob Servant
Subject: ATTENTION MR. BOB

Attention: Mr Bob Servant,
Well I received your mail but let me ask, who gave you my email?
Anyway, I am Mr Randy Whyting from WESTBROOK USA and in
fact it is a terrible thing. I trusted JIMJAMS in helping him by putting
his money into my account and I will take 20%. He and his group
collaborated with a bank of Africa to collect my $72,000 and disappear.

 My dear, the funniest thing is that this man use to dress like a woman!
And he used to plate long hair according to the photo that he send when
the transaction is going. I promised the police if they capture him i pay
$12,500. I have heard the man has been captured and so I am going to go
immediately with the money that i promised. I am also going to Dakar for
the rest of my money. If you are also a victim like this, I advise you to do
similar, that is the truth.

Thanks

Mr Randy Whyting

WESTBROOK USA.

From: Bob Servant
To: Randy Whyting
Subject: Hello Randy

Hi Randy,
Thanks so much for getting in touch. You sound a little familiar, have we
met before? I am deeply sorry you have also become a victim of JIMJAMS
who you probably call a coyote in American. It's interesting he had long
hair in the photo he sent you. The bit about women's clothes I think is a
mix-up at your end but never mind that for now. Do you have an American
landline I could call you on? Also, please send the photo of Jimjams. We
should stay together in the hotel over there. We could curl up with a real
weepy?

Many thanks,

Bob

From: Randy Whyting
To: Bob Servant
Subject: ATTENTION MR BOB

Attn: Bob,
What up my man. I do not have the photo now as I deleted everything
in my email but my lawyer in Dakar is a registered lawyer so he cannot
tell me lies. My man I will be moving to Dakar as i told you. Concerning
phone do not ask me about my phone because I do not know you before.
Let us wait to meet in Dakar so we can see over each and get to know
more better my man.

Bye

Mr Randy Whyting

From: Bob Servant
To: Randy Whyting
Subject: Good Old Randy

Hi Randy,
What up my man? I love the way that you Americans speak, it's so
distinctive. When are you flying over there Randy? How are you going to
get from the ranch to the airport? Any chance of a photo of you? Not in a
saucy way.

Bob

From: Randy Whyting
To: Bob Servant
Subject: OK

Attn: Bob Servant,
How are you, my man? Please stop this bullshit about photo. Let us meet
in Dakar and talk then. I am going there now and you should do the
same if you do not want to lose your money. My friend all I know is that
Jimjams is captured so let us go and get our money,

Bye

Randy

From: Bob Servant
To: Youssou Ba
Subject: FW: OK

Youssou,

Jesus, what's going on with Randy? Check out the email attached. The
guy sounds like a loose cannon. I don't think I want to come and share
a hotel room with this lunatic. All I asked for was a photo and I made
it abundantly clear I didn't want it in a saucy way. I think we've landed
ourselves a real, old-time cowboy in Randy and I for one don't want to be
around when he comes a-walking through the saloon doors. Fuck that. I'm
out.

Bob

From: Youssou Ba
To: Bob Servant
Subject: re:Randy

Dear Mr Bob,

My dear do not be upset by the American. I hear that he is a retired
military man and his age now is 79 yrs ok. I need you to tell me that
you are coming to claim your money and you are going to send the
Gendarmerie the money that you owe them through Western Union. I am
totally disappointed with you just now,

Sincerely

Mr Youssou Ba

GENDARMERIE

From: Bob Servant
To: Randy Whyting
Subject: I have been a fool

Randy,

I think I owe you an apology. You should have said earlier that you were so
old, Youssou just told me. I had no idea. Perhaps that's why your English
isn't so good? Listen, I hope that your journey goes well and I look forward
to seeing you over there. I get there on Wednesday evening.

Many thanks,

Bob

From: Bob Servant
To: Youssou Ba
Subject: Back on track, clothing

Youssou,
All sorted with Randy. I didn't realise he was so old or I would have been more understanding. I am now fully satisfied with things. I am going to go to the travel agent tomorrow and confirm my flights. I'm worried about the heat. I have been offered two travelling outfits. One by Tommy Peanuts who is suggesting I borrow his jogging outfit and one by Frank's nephew who played Dr Livingstone in his school play. It was a great production. They gave a carry-out to a janitor at Ninewells Zoo and managed to get a lion in for it.[33] Photos of the outfits are attached. Which one would you like to see me in? And hold me in, when we are alone in the hotel?

Bob

From: Youssou Ba
To: Bob Servant
Subject: When do you come?

Dear Mr Bob Servant,
I will not be in your hotel I will be at home with my wife and children OK now? I think you should wear the blue outfit and this will be good as

---

33. The staff of Dundee's Ninewells Zoo are both highly trained and dedicated. The idea that one would accept a bribe of alcohol (or anything else for that matter) to look the other way while members of the public borrowed a lion is outrageous.

then you will stand out at the airport. You must send the £2,500 now or at the very least bring the £5,000 cash for the airport.

Sincerely

Mr Youssou Ba

GENDARMERIE

From: Bob Servant
To: Youssou Ba
Subject: A Special Request

Youssou,
One last request. I'd like to go on an off-road safari whilst there and wondered if you and your men would provide security? There will be lots of wild animals about (hopefully!) so you could ride on the roof of the van and, if any charge us, you would pick them off with potshots? I will be able to pass sandwiches up to you through the car windows, unless there are too many animals about as they might get the scent and take my arm off. It's hardly worth losing an arm for a sandwich? I am willing to pay you $100 a day for this security work. Please let me know if you accept, and also what kind of sandwiches you require. Many thanks, and happy hunting!

Bob

From: Youssou Ba
To: Bob Servant
Subject: I will arrange

Attn; Mr Bob
Kind to hear from you, I will be glad to receive you. For your security you don't have any problem on the safari and also when not on the safari. We will eat before we come to work also. So feel free as you will rejoice when you will come down, confirm the flight name and number for me now. But you are dribbling me like a kid, saying you will come today, tomorrow? Please send the £2,500 in mean time?

Sincerely

Mr Youssou Ba

GENDARMERIE

From: Bob Servant
To: Dr. Youssou Ba
Subject: Why the long face?

Youssou,

I would never dribble you like a kid. I have confirmed the flight and need to leave right now. Chappy Williams is taking me in his Sierra to Edinburgh Airport then I fly to Paris and then on to your country. I will email you from Paris, Chappy's son is showing me how to work his Blackberry so I will give it my best shot.[34] As far as I'm concerned, if Randy can fly to Africa at the age of 79 then I can learn how to use a Blackberry at 63. He's an inspiration to us all, is old Randy Whyting.

I am wearing the blue travelling outfit as you requested. How will I know who you are at the airport on Saturday? Maybe you could wear something similar?

Bob

From: Youssou Ba
To: Bob Servant
Subject: OK

Dear Mr Bob Servant ,
Good. I will try to match. Please remember the £5,000 cash.

Sincerely

Mr Youssou Ba

GENDARMERIE

From: Bob Servant
To: Dr. Mamadou Kouassi, Youssou Ba
Subject: FROM PARIS AIRPORT

Sent from my Blackberry

Doctor Marmalade and Youssou,
Hola my friends and greetings from Paris on the Blackberry! See you both at the airport I hope? Matching up to my travelling outfit is a really nice

---

34. For me, this is the most outlandish note in the entire, sorry collection of Bob Servant's emails. The idea that he could operate a Blackberry device is complete insanity. He covers his microwave with a blanket while it's operating and was told by Chappy Williams that he could only make mobile phone calls from within public phoneboxes, a practice he maintained for nearly the whole of 2002.

touch. Not only will it make it easier to identify each other but it will make us feel closer to each other. Isn't it funny that, after all this time, we are about to finally meet? My flight details are below, I cannot wait to arrive.

DEPART - HEATHROW - 1700
ARRIVE - PARIS - 2200
DEPART - PARIS - 0800
ARRIVE - DHAKA - 1730
FLIGHT NO AZ675436
BANGLADESHI AIRLINES
COST - $1764.45

See you tomorrow in Dhaka,

All the very best,

Bob

From: Dr. Mamadou Kouassi
To: Bob Servant
Subject: OK

Dear Bob,
Thank you for the information and I will keep on waiting at the airport for your arrival here in Dakar. It is Dakar not Dhaka. I am Mamadou.

Bye and God bless.

Dr.Mamadou.

From: Bob Servant
To: Dr. Mamadou Kouassi
Subject: FROM PARIS AIRPORT

Sent From My Blackberry

Marmalade,
We're just boarding. A slight delay, the flight will now arrive in Dhaka at 1830. I have changed my money into Takas and I will see you at the airpot in Dhaka tonight. Ok, got to go. See you soon my friend. My love to Youssou and Randy,

Bob

From: Dr. Mamadou Kouassi
To: Bob Servant
Subject: Dakar

DEAR BOB,
THANK YOU BUT IT IS DAKAR FOR THE PLANE YOU ARE TO
GET

THANK YOU.

From: Bob Servant
To: Dr. Mamadou Kouassi
Subject: You What?

Sent from my Blackberry

Dr Marmalade,
We have landed to refuel in Turkey. What is Dakar? I am going to Dhaka, I
thought that was where you lived? That's the plane moving again, I arrive
in Dhaka in a few hours. Will you be there to meet me? How is Randy?

Bob

From: Dr. Mamadou Kouassi
To: Bob Servant
Subject: What do you mean?

BOB
IT SEEMS YOU ARE JOKING WITH ME? HAVE I TOLD YOU OF
DHAKA EVER? I TOLD YOU DAKAR CAPITAL OF SENEGAL
WEST AFRICA. IN FACT I DON'T UNDERSTAND YOUR POINT?
ENTER AIR FRANCE TO DAKAR OK. DO IT NOW BOB.

THANK YOU

DR. MAMADOU.

From: Bob Servant
To: Dr. Mamadou Kouassi
Subject: Eh?

Sent from my Blackberry

How am I meant to change planes? We're at 40,000 feet. I'm not fucking
James Bond.

From: Dr. Mamadou Kouassi
To: Bob Servant
Subject: re: Eh?

ENTER AIR FRANCE TO DAKAR IMMEDIATELY

From: Bob Servant
To: Dr. Mamadou Kouassi
Subject: What have you done to me?

Marmalade,
I have just landed in Dhaka and, quite frankly, I am absolutely furious with
you. Why the hell did you tell me that you lived in Dhaka if you wanted
me to come to Senegal? I've wound up in Bangladesh. As if things can't
get any worse, you and Youssou told me to wear this bloody outfit. It's
absolutely fucking roasting here. I feel like my balls are on fire, the lycra
is stuck fast and I'm losing the circulation to my legs. I have booked into
a hotel and am going to stay overnight while I work out what to do next. Is
there any way that you can get a flight over here and meet me? Christ, I
wish I'd brought other clothes.

Bob

PS Is Randy ok?

From: Dr. Mamadou Kouassi
To: Bob Servant
Subject: From Dr. Mamadou

Dear Bob,
Mamadou. I thank you for your mail. I myself is totally confused and I do
not know what to do but the only advice I am giving is to board now from
the Dhaka back to Paris France and stop at their international air port and
then enter Air France or any flight that is coming to DAKAR CAPITAL
OF SENEGAL in West Africa immediately without wasting time.

My friend do not be discouraged it is the mistake that you made
because i always specify everything right from the begining till today, so
more grease to your elbow, just keep on. I got information that Mr Randy
arrived and the GENDARMERIE told me it now looks like JIMJAMS
will pay up all the money he stole from you and the American Randy
Whyting. I advice you start coming and keep me posted but concerning

your clothes if they are now no good then we go directly to purchase new materials.

Awaiting your reply urgently.

By now.

Dr. Mamadou Kouassi.

From: Bob Servant
To: Dr. Mamadou Kouassi
Subject: Things are picking up

Marmalade,
How are you my friend? I am having a great time here in Dhaka. At first I wasn't too happy (as you probably noticed!) but I decided to give it a chance and I'm really glad I did. Last night I went to a bar and, well, I've kind of met someone.

His name is KAZI and he works at the bar as a bouncer. His English is quite good and we got to chatting and I guess it just clicked. I don't want to get carried away, but I must admit that I do really, really like him. He is a strong man who is not scared to give his opinions and I admire that. He is also a sensational lover.

I am going to stay here with KAZI for a while. The two of us are hiring a caravan tomorrow and he is taking me on a tour of his country. He wants to take me to his hometown and show me off. Imagine someone wanting to show off silly old Bob! Oh Doctor Marmalade, am I being a fool? Is there such a thing as love at first sight or is KAZI playing me for a bellend? Here is a photo of KAZI. I hope you like him, I'm crazy about the big lump.

I will keep you posted, wish me luck!

Bob

From: Dr. Mamadou Kouassi
To: Bob Servant
Subject: Are you coming or not?

Dear Bob,

Thank you for your mail and i will like to welcome you in my country here DAKAR IN SENEGAL WEST AFRICA but tell me when i will be expecting you? Or can you send just £500 now through Western Union and I will hold your money for you with no further charges? Your friend can come to DAKAR with you.

Awaiting your reply.

Dr Mamadou.

From: Bob Servant
To: Dr. Mamadou Kouassi, Youssou Ba, Randy Whyting
Subject: Look out your party gear!

Bob and Kazi's Special Day

You're invited!

Host-Bob and Kazi

Location Dhaka Church, Dhaka High Street, Dhaka

Time-Saturday, June 24, 12:00pm

Gentlemen of Senegal and America. My newly found man of my dreams, Kazi, and I would like to invite you to our wedding here in Dhaka. If it was not for you I would never have found myself here and would not have met Kazi at the Happy Kiss Bar. It would be fantastic if the three of you could make it to the wedding next Saturday. The dress code is OuTRAGEOuS. We want the day to be a celebration of our love and a really good knees-up. I hope that you can get time off from the hospital and the police station, and that Randy can extend his trip. It won't be the same without the three of you because you're such distinctive, completely separate characters.

Yours forever,
Bob

NO REPLY/THE END

8
From Lanzhou to Willy's Chinese Palace

From: LANZHOU GLOBAL LTD
To: Bob Servant
Subject: JOB OPPORTUNITY/ MAKE MORE INCOME

Dear Sir/Madam,
We are Lanzhou Global, a specialist in the production of Rubber belts
such as power transmission belts, conveyor belts etc. We have reached
big sales volume of rubber products in USA/Canada and now trying to
penetrate the United Kingdom and European market. Quite soon we shall
open representative offices in the United Kingdom and therefore we are
looking for people to assist us.

   We need agents to receive payment in bank wire transfers and to
resend the money to us. You earn 10% from each operation and work
as an independent contractor right from your home office. Your job is
absolutely legal. You can earn up to 3000–4000 pounds monthly.

Best Regards,

Admin/Human Resources Manager, Xiong Li.

From: Bob Servant
To: LANZHOU GLOBAL LTD
Subject: OK, let's talk

Hello there
This looks very interesting indeed. My name is Bob Servant and I am a
semi-retired window cleaner. How would I go about applying for this job?

Your Servant,

Bob Servant

From: LANZHOU GLOBAL LTD
To: Bob Servant
Subject: JOB OPPORTUNITY/ MAKE MORE INCOME

Dear Bob,
Thanks for responding to our offer. We are pleased with your interest.
We are looking to extend our business to United Kingdom and have been
facing difficulties in handling payments from our client, that is why we
have decided to employ people over there whom we can trust. Do you
understand our aims OK? Do not hesitate to ask any question.

XIONG LI

From: Bob Servant
To: LANZHOU GLOBAL LTD
Subject: MY GARAGE COULD BE AN OFFICE

Xiong,

I am very interested in working for your company. I have a big garage that I do not use much and I was thinking that I could convert it into an office? The only thing is that it is absolutely freezing in there because I knocked a hole in the wall once when I decided that I needed an escape tunnel from the house. Looking back it was a stupid decision but it was around the time of the Millennium Bug and a lot of people were panicking. I remember wee Jane at Mrs. Muffin's being too scared to use their till on New Year's Day because Chappy Williams told her it might explode.

There isn't much in the garage – just a bike, a barbecue and about 30,000 jazz mags.

Many thanks,

Bob

PS What would be my job title?

PPS Is there a uniform?

From: LANZHOU GLOBAL LTD
To: Bob Servant
Subject: Re: MY GARAGE COULD BE AN OFFICE

Hello Bob,

Thanks a lot. Listen Bob this job does not require your much time or space. It's lucrative but all we need is you handling and collecting payments from our clients.You do not need a uniform for this and get 10% of each payment. You can give yourself any title you want. Please give us your full personal and banking details so we can get started with this now Bob,

Thanks,

Xiong

From: Bob Servant
To: LANZHOU GLOBAL LTD
Subject: Thoughts on a uniform

Xiong,

I am an old-fashioned kind of man and as far as I'm concerned if you are working then you wear a uniform, it's as simple as that. Perhaps it would

be possible for me to arrange a uniform over here and show you to see
if it ties in with your corporate image? What kind of look do you go for
yourself? Do you wear a suit or a branded tracksuit?

I want something tight, that's vital. It makes me feel alert. I remember
when I still had the windowcleaning round. Whenever we had a bumper
day I used to wear two pairs of pants, tight ones too and sometimes stick
a dishcloth down there as well. I walked about the place like a bloody
cowboy but it really put me in the zone. I remember the boys down at
Toshy's Hardware used to encourage me. One time a few of them stuck
me in the shop window and managed to get eight towels down my pants
and trousers while everyone clapped outside.[35]

With regards to the information you need about old Bob here, can you
please be a bit more specific. I have had a long and fruitful life Xiong, and
if I'm going to open that can of worms then God only knows what could
pop out! Your new employee, a proud member of the Lanzhou Team,

The Big Man,

Bob Servant

From: LANZHOU GLOBAL LTD
To: Bob Servant
Subject: APPLICATION FORM

Hello Big Man!
We are glad to have you as our staff, this is the information that we need.
Do what you think is best for a uniform Bob. We trust you. I wear a suit.

PERSONAL DETAILS

First Name:
Middle Name:
Last Name:
Date Of Birth:
Sex:
Occupation:
Marital Status:
National Insurance Number/Social Security Number:
Address:

City:
State:
Zip/Postal Code:
Country:

----

35. A quick call to Toshy's Hardware in Broughty Ferry unsurprisingly confirms
that this incident did not take place.

Home Phone:
Mobile Phone:
Fax:

CERTIFICATION:
I hereby certify that all entries are true and complete. I agree and understand that any falsification of information, regardless of time of discovery, may cause forfeiture on my part of employment in the service of Lanzhou Global Manufacturing Co. Ltd. I consent to criminal history background checks.

Date:

Applicant Signature:

OFFICIAL USE ONLY:

Remarks:

Lanzhou Global Manufacturing Co., Ltd.

████████████████
████████████████
████████████████

Thailand.

From: Bob Servant
To: LANZHOU GLOBAL LTD
Subject: UNIFORMS

Xiong,
Hello boss! I have been trying like a bastard to find the right uniform for the job and I think I have it - a boilersuit that I bought for £30 from Nipper Kolacz, who works at the Michelin. Nipper wasn't able to give me a receipt because they get given them free but could I still claim it on expenses?

Here's what I want to do with it. On the front left chest pocket I want to put my initials – BGS – like what football managers have on their training jackets. It's on the back that I want to get a little bit saucy. I don't know if you have a slogan over there at LANZHOU GLOBAL LTD or not but I have come up with one that I think is a bit of a cracker.

Are you ready?

HEY DICKHEAD! ARE YOU LAUGHING AT OUR RUBBER? SHUT UP OR WE'LL BELT YOU!

(And then underneath that) - LANZHOU GLOBAL - THE BEST RUBBER BELTS IN THE WORLD.

What do you think? It's quite long so the writing would have to be pretty small but I think it sets the right tone. It's extremely funny but also presents us as a serious international rubber belt company.

One final thing, are we going to advertise the fact that we have touched down in Scotland? I was up in Fintry the other day looking for skirt and I saw a cracking advertising board. I took a photo of it to show you as I thought it would be a great spot for a LANZHOU GLOBAL LTD advert – maybe using my new slogan? Let me know what you think, it's got a car on it just now but it's not a real car so it would be easy to take it off.

I've really enjoyed my first two days of working for LANZHOU GLOBAL LTD. It's been all go, but I have had a great time. I'll get to grips with the form tomorrow.

This is Bob Servant, star man of Lanzhou Global Ltd, clocking off!

Yours loyally,

Barbara

From: LANZHOU GLOBAL LTD
To: Bob Servant
Subject: Form needed

Dear Bob,
I am glad to read your message, I am very impressed with you and I must say you might be one of our best staff because of your good attitude and loyalty. I am proud of you and I feel you can help us have a large market in the UK. The uniform sounds perfect. You should wear it when you are doing your business as you will look smart. Let us have a think about what advertisements we might do but you have made a good start.

Bob, do not hesitate to send back your job application form. It is very important and we need this information for our system. We also have clients that will start making payments into your banking account very soon,

XIONG

From: Bob Servant
To: LANZHOU GLOBAL LTD
Subject: Completed Form (stick it in your pipe and smoke it!) (only joking) (though you can if you want) (don't choke to death without paying me though!) (only joking)

Xiong,

I've done the form! Isn't this incredible Xiong, old Bobby boy working for a Chinese belt company?! But why not? The thing is Xiong, you're over there in China and I'm here in Broughty Ferry. But you're just a man and I'm just a man. That's what I'm saying. We're all just men. Apart from women.

All the very, very best,

Sandra

JOB APPLICATION FORM
PERSONAL DETAILS

First Name: BOB
Middle Name: GODZILLA
Last Name: SERVANT
Date Of Birth: 62 YEARS OLD DO NOT CELEBRATE BIRTHDAY
                   BECAUSE OF STRESS OF ORGANISING PARTY
Sex: MALE (100%)
Occupation: SCOTTISH REPRESENTATIVE FOR LANZHOU
                   GLOBAL LTD
Marital Status: SINGLE/AVAILABLE
National Insurance Number/Social Security Number: WOULD RATHER
                   WORK CASH IN HAND PLEASE
Address: 18 HARBOUR VIEW City: DUNDEE State: TAYSIDE
                   Zip/Postal Code: ZIP? Country: SCOTLAND
Home Phone: BROKEN
Mobile Phone: GOT ONE FOR CHRISTMAS FROM TOMMY
                   PEANUTS BUT LOST IN BET ON BOXING DAY (ARM
                   WRESTLE WITH TOMMY PEANUTS)[36]

---

36. Bob does, in actual fact, possess a mobile phone that he calls 'The Batphone'. For the first six months he owned it, Bob used his phone only while standing in phone boxes after Chappy Williams told him that they were the only locations that offered a signal for his particular model.

Fax: I THINK THE POST OFFICE HAS ONE THAT I COULD
                    USE?

CERTIFICATION:

I hereby certify that all entries are true and complete. I agree and
understand that any falsification of information, regardless of time of
discovery, may cause forfeiture on my part of employment in the service
of Lanzhou Global Manufacturing Co. Ltd. I consent to criminal history
background checks.

Date: 28/3/07

Applicant Signature: Bobby Servant. By the way, about those checks,
I smoked a few Fatty Boom Booms in the late 1970s but I never really
enjoyed them that much. Other than that, you'll probably dig up some bits
and pieces but they all resulted from genuine misunderstandings.

FOR OFFICIAL USE ONLY:

Remarks: BOB IS A GOOD GUY

From: LANZHOU GLOBAL LTD
To: Bob Servant
Subject : MISSING INFORMATION

Hello Bob,
Thank you for sending the form but it is not totally correct. You did not
give us your postal address and no national insurance number. Kindly do
that and meanwhile one of our clients is ready to make a payment so we
need your phone number and bank details soon,

Thank You,

XIONG

From: Bob Servant
To: LANZHOU GLOBAL LTD
Subject: STAFF PARTY

Xiong,
Thanks you for your email. You know, Xiong, when I hear from you, my
special boss with his kind words, I feel about ten feet tall. It's lucky I'm not
though, or I wouldn't be able to get into my house! I would, of course, I
could just crawl in the front door or lever myself through a window. Either
way, I'd get into the house. That's for bloody sure.
    Xiong, I have been very, very busy. I know you want to get these forms
done but it's not all about paperwork in business Xiong, you should know

that. What we need Xiong, is to let people know that we are here and we mean business. Rubber belt business.

I've started spreading the word locally in Broughty Ferry, and then I'll take it on a rolling campaign through Douglas and Mid Craigie, up the Kingsway and back through the West End to the city centre. People are intrigued and welcoming to the company and they're fascinated by where we want to take it.

I have also been thinking about a staff night out. Obviously, as things stand there is just me here in the Scottish office, but I was thinking of inviting a couple of people. The first guy I thought of was Clive from the Royal Bank.[37] Clive is a bit eccentric but is also quite senior I think. He's a good guy and he could be quite important to us for setting up bank accounts and so on. The other one is Hamish McAlpine, the former Dundee United goalkeeper. Hamish is a distinctive local character and a good guy to have onside. I have attached a photo.

With regards to locations, then I think that Chinese would be the most appropriate as I'm sure you agree! Ha, ha. Probably the best Chinese in Broughty Ferry is Willy's Chinese Palace. They do a good dinner deal for under a tenner so if Clive, Hamish and myself all have that and maybe two bottles of wine then you'd be talking about £40–£50 for the whole thing.

Is that OK? Shall I just keep a receipt and send it over to you?

Anyway, I'd better be off. I've got a major marketing plan for the next few days, which I will tell you about later. I'm hoping to surprise you with some great news.

Your Faithful Employee and Friend,

Bob Servant

------

37. Bob originally refused to tell me if Clive exists. Having spent two days ascertaining that no Clive has ever worked at any Broughty Ferry bank, Bob then admitted he has never met anyone called Clive. He generously added that he does know a Cliff, a man who he describes as 'a total clown'.

From: LANZHOU GLOBAL LTD
To: Bob Servant
Subject: Information Bob

Bob,

Thank you again for your hard work for the company. I think that the party is a good idea and yes we would prefer you to eat at a Chinese restaurant as we are a Chinese company originally. But Bob you have still not given us your national insurance number, bank account information and phone number right away. You said that Tommy broke your phone have you not got another one?

Also, we cannot find a record of your address, have you written it properly?

Please hurry Bob

Xiong

From: Bob Servant
To: LANZHOU GLOBAL LTD
Subject: Will the rain affect the belts?

Xiong,

My address is 18 Harbour View, Broughty Ferry. It's the house with the long grass, next but one to the house with the greenhouse. That's Frank Theplank's house. You might have heard that he used to work with me at a cafe I had but the whole thing turned to shit. We're back talking now but for a while it was purely nods and winks.

I do have a National Insurance number, it is ██████████. However, I would really not want to get the Government involved in this whole kettle of Chinese fish. I have not paid any taxes since '89 and that was by mistake and because I was sitting pretty from the cheeseburger vans and half-mad at the time.

Unfortunately I do not have a phone right now. A few months ago I went absolutely berserk on Booty Express but it turned out it was costing me £1 a bloody minute. I couldn't believe it, I thought they were joking when they said that stuff at the beginning of the call. The girls were quality, Xiong, real good time girls with very few hang-ups. We had some great times but then I got the bill through and it was nearly £300. One thing led to another and I took out the phone with a spanner.

Do you want me to get a new one for the business? There's a nice one in the Argos Catalogue for £8.99 but my Argos Catalogue is three years old so you can probably stick a fiver on top of that.

Things have been going really well with getting people talking about the business. One thing though, a lot of people are excited but ask me the same question - What do the rubber belts look like and how much are they going to cost? There is some resistance from the usual suspects. In the Post Office bar the other day Chappy Williams said, "Why would I wear a rubber belt Bob, I'd look like a prick" and then, in The Anchor, Tommy Peanuts said that rubber belts would shrink in the rain and cut off the circulation to your legs.

I thought that was a fair point actually, is it true?

By the way, the staff party is booked for Willy's Chinese Palace. I nipped in earlier and reserved a table for three, and Hamish and Clive are both confirmed. Chick Devine, the barman at Stewpot's, is cousins with Hamish and says he'll definitely be there. I went to the bank and confirmed with Clive as well. He went all weird, bright red and saying how excited he was and stuff. He's a weirdo, I hope he's not going to be an idiot at the party.

Your best worker,

Bob Servant

From: **LANZHOU GLOBAL LTD**
To: **Bob Servant**
Subject: **Thank you Bob**

Bob,

How are you? Thank you for the information. We are now going to set up the first payment to you of £3,000. You can take £300 commission from this as reward for all your hard work. You can also take the money for the party at Willy's Palace. We would like you to have a good time at the party so will pay what you need in extra commission.

So now Bob we just need your bank information. Please send this so I can have everything set up,

Thanks you and well done,

Xiong

From: **Bob Servant**
To: **LANZHOU GLOBAL LTD**
Subject: **PARTY TIME FOR LANZHOU!**

Xiong,

Well, this is it, the day of the LANZHOU GLOBAL LIMITED (SCOTLAND) staff night out. I am so excited Xiong. The last staff party I went to was when I still had the windowcleaning round and I took the boys up to

Godden's Goodtime Girls in Dundee for some tabledancing. Christ, that was a disaster. The two women that came out looked as if they were the bloody cleaners and they were so clumsy about everything it was hard to relax. In fact, now I come to think of it, they might well have been the cleaners. It was only half past ten in the morning.

I remember when we got back down the Ferry we told Father O'Neill about it and he was pissing himself laughing, joking about how he was going to take the church mob there for their Christmas do. He's a good guy Father O'Neill. He always gets his round in and he's honest too. He once admitted to me and Tommy Peanuts that the Bible's a lot of bollocks and he's only in the game for the free accomodation.[38]

Anyway, I'm sure tonight will be a big success. I popped my head through the door at Stewpot's and shouted over to Chick Devine if Hamish was definitely going to be there. He said "Yeah, that's right Bob, Hamish McAlpine's going to your party" and everyone laughed, but that's just because they're jealous.

Listen, Xiong, I am going to speak to Clive at the party about the banking needs for LANZHOU GLOBAL. What kind of account do I need? I'm not bothered, as long as I get one of those plastic card holders. Tommy Peanuts has one and he's forever flashing it about. The way he lets the thing fall open at the bar you'd think he was from the fucking FBI.

Your faithful employee and one of your best friends,

Daphne

From: LANZHOU GLOBAL LTD
To: Bob Servant
Subject: RE: PARTY TIME FOR LANZHOU!

Hello BOB,
We are a little concerned as we checked your name and address on the UK directory online but we could not find it. So how do we know you are whom you claim to be? Also this is no joke, this is a job offer and we want you to take it serious. We have clients who want to make payment with cheque and balance transfer but we are afraid that it seems the details you gave is incorrect and you are not taking us serious.
We hope you are not a joke Bob. Kindly mail back.

XIONG

---

38. I should clarify that the figure of 'Father O'Neill' is not based on any past or present representative of any religious organisation, in Broughty Ferry or elsewhere.

From: Bob Servant
To: LANZHOU GLOBAL LTD
Subject: Party, Address

Xiong, I have some bad news, which I will come to shortly, but first I want to voice my deep anger. Xiong, are you calling me a liar? The only way that business can work is with 100% honesty and that is what I have given you.

I am ex-directory because five years ago I stole a wheelbarrow and several potted plants from Dawson Park. I was worried that the council were in cahoots with BT for stuff like that so went ex-directory. I wish you had asked what was going on rather than jump to conclusions and try me in a kangaroo court. You are behaving like Adolf Hitler. That said, I entirely forgive you.

I do, however, have bad news. The party was a disaster. First, Hamish McAlpine didn't turn up. It turns out Chick Devine doesn't know Hamish at all. He's a stupid liar who thinks he's funny. The only thing that made me think they're cousins is that Chick has a moustache as well but that doesn't really mean anything does it? Especially when you look at the fact I've never seen Chick and Hamish together and that they don't look alike. And that Chick's black.

So, anyway, Hamish didn't show and Clive totally misunderstood the whole thing and thought me and him were going on some sort of bloody date. Xiong, the guy turned up in a fucking dress and makeup. I walked in and thought there was no-one there apart from some rough bird and then looked again and it was actually Clive. I had brought along a few belts and a speech but it was all a waste of time. Clive started nicking all the prawn crackers and things got a bit out of hand.

The police came, which was a total overreaction. Someone grassed to the Evening Telegraph and they (surprise, surprise) stuck it in today. I've been getting pelters about what happened and all the stuff with Clive. Everyone keeps asking me where my boyfriend is and if I'm off up to the bank to kiss him. I popped into Stewpot's for lunch and the boys in there gave it - 'Oooh, did Clive let you open his account Bob' and 'Don't be jealous Bob, but I was up the bank earlier and I caught Clive fiddling with some coppers'.

That last one made me laugh to be honest. Then Chappy Williams got in trouble trying to do something with 'overdrafts'. It was brilliant. He said, 'Ooh did Clive give you an overdraft Bob?' and I just said, 'How's that funny Chappy?' and everyone laughed at him, so that was not too bad. I just finished my pie and left after that.

Anyway, I'll attach the article. They've always had it in for me, ever since I was interviewed on Radio Tay at the Broughty Ferry gala week and the reporter asked if I read about the Evening Telegraph saying the gala week was the worst ever and I said that I only ever bought the Evening Telegraph if the Spar has sold out of toilet paper. It wasn't my joke (it was one of Frank Theplanks though, when he said it, I'm not sure if he was joking).[39] The paper have been on my back ever since. They're always throwing in the thing about my ladders being nicked and how it wasn't gypsies that stole them. It definitely was.

Your loyal employee,

Bob Servant

PS here's the article –

Dundee Evening Telegraph
Broughty Ferry News   28-03-07

Filed 01.04.07 by Broughty Ferry Breaking News Team

CHINESE COMPANY'S CHRISTMAS NIGHT OUT ENDS IN FARCICAL SCENES

Chaos reigned at a Broughty Ferry restaurant last night when two local men celebrated a Christmas night out that ended with one of them tying the other to a postbox and force-feeding him prawn crackers. The victim, who was dressed in women's clothing and has asked not to be named, required medical treatment at the scene by paramedics in what police described today as 'a moment of madness' from the attacker, Robert Servant (62) of Harbour View Road.

The night, sponsored by Chinese company Lanzhou Global Development Ltd, for whom Mr Servant is Director of Operations (Scotland), got off to a bizarre beginning according to witnesses. When Mr Servant arrived at Willy's Chinese Palace restaurant in Gray Street, he was 'astonished' to see his fellow diner sitting waiting for him, according to manager Willie Yuan.

'Mr Servant, who we have had trouble with before, went berserk,' said Mr Yuan this morning. 'He started shouting, "What the hell's up with your get up? Why are you wearing a f**king dress?" And then he was saying, "Where's Hamish? Where's Hamish?" It was very frightening indeed and it was a relief when he finally sat down.'

The staff say they were too

---

39. After an exhaustive search of Radio Tay's transcripts for every Broughty Ferry Gala Week for the past twenty years, no record of this conversation can be found. I confidently state that the *Evening Telegraph* made no such claim about the much-admired Broughty Ferry Gala Week, and Bob Servant made no such claim about his less-admired bottom.

scared to tackle Mr Servant who then proceeded to dine in silence with his companion, a situation seemingly ended when Mr Servant felt that he had been cheated out of his share of the communal bowl of prawn crackers.

'That was when things got completely out of hand,' said Mr Yuan. 'The two of them started shouting and fighting and it spilled out onto the street. Mr Servant seemed to have a number of men's belts with him and he used these to tie his friend to the postbox. Then he ran back in and stole some bags of prawn crackers and went back outside.

'We locked the doors but we could see him stuffing the crackers into his friend's mouth and that was when we called the police. He was shouting, "Happy now? Happy now?" It was terrifying. I told the waiter to close the curtains and we didn't open them until we heard the sirens.'

Mr Servant was arrested at the scene but later released when the victim of the attack refused to press charges. A police spokesman today confirmed that Mr Servant was known to them and his future behaviour would be observed. Mr Servant was not available for comment and his house showed little signs of life while Lanzhou Global Development Ltd could not be traced at the time of going to press.[40]

From: LANZHOU GLOBAL LTD
To: Bob Servant
Subject: I am sorry Bob

Hello Bob,

I am very sorry. I am only doing my job and asking you the questions that the company's personnel manager is telling me to ask you. I know that you are OK Bob, but they have told me to ask. We need to know if the details given to us are for real.

A client wants to make payment with balance transfer. You know what this is? So he needs your credit card long number and the limit so he can make the payment on it. Also can I know which bank you use? I know there is now a problem with Clive so let me know what bank you will use.

Do not worry about the party. Sometimes when men are together things happen that no-one is proud of. The newspaper will forget about it I am sure as have the police. That is more important as you cannot work for us in jail!

Thanks

Xiong

----

40. After a slightly less taxing search, it can be established that this article never appeared in the *Evening Telegraph*.

From: Bob Servant
To: LANZHOU GLOBAL LTD
Subject: IT'S OVER

Xiong,

My friend. I hope that you can see my reasons for saying what I am about to say. We've had some good times together. We've laughed and joked and worked damn hard to get LANZHOU GLOBAL LTD the respect that it undoubtedly deserves. I love the company Xiong and, in many ways, I love you. But things change my friend. Sometimes life just grabs you by the balls and whispers 'think again compadre' whilst stroking your neck.

Xiong, I'll be honest with you, I'm holding up my hands and taking on the long walk. I know what you might think, that old Bob here has lost his bottle. That ten years ago Bob Servant would have turned round to the critics of LANZHOU GLOBAL LTD and told them to shut it, that we were going to show them we meant business and that, come the summer, every man and his dog in Dundee would be wearing one of our rubber belts. And you know what, Xiong, maybe you'd be right. Maybe you'd be right.

It's the paper Xiong, the bloody paper. That's what whored it for us. They just kept on my bloody back, coming round and ringing the bell and shouting 'come on Mr Servant, we only want a quick word'. But they didn't just want a quick word Xiong. They wanted their pound of flesh and, this afternoon, I suppose that's just what they got.

I was down at the Fisherman's Bar when I heard that they were in a bidding war with the Gazette for Clive's side of the story, 'My Chinese Horror', that he was demanding £25 for. I don't think he would have gone through with it. He doesn't have the guts and would have had to live in hiding somewhere I wouldn't track him down. Invergowrie, or even through in Perth.

Anyway, I decided that enough was enough. I spoke to Pop Wood who told me that legally, the best advice he could give me was to 'see the thing off at the pass' and speak to the Evening Telegraph myself. Pop is a great lawyer, though he's struck off for giving a false alibi to Tommy Peanuts when he vandalised Sally Peanut's new husband's Renault Laguna outside Maciocia's chip shop. That's why he's in the Fisherman's all the time I suppose.

So I called up the Evening Telegraph vipers and told them to come down. We cleaned the dominoes table and stuck it in the beer garden. Pop gave me a tie that he had in his briefcase (he carries it all the time because his wife doesn't know he's been struck off). I put on his glasses but they gave me a sore head so I took them off. I made a little sign out of the back of one of the menus and wrote 'BOB SERVANT STRIKES BACK' on it and propped it up in front of me.

Then I sat and composed myself with a gin and juice while Pop waited in the bar. I could hear him say 'Mr Servant will see you now' and he led the journalist through to the beer garden. Things went not too badly, I attach the article below. They managed to get in the thing about the ladders, which I knew they would, but they didn't really twist my words like the press can.

And that's that I suppose Xiong. I'd like to place on record how much I have enjoyed my time working with LANZHOU GLOBAL LTD. We've had a great wee spell and I have certainly done what I can to spread word throughout the Dundee area. At the very least Xiong, people will give you a chance.

I suppose this is goodbye Xiong. Oh, God, I can't believe I'm writing these words. I'm going to stop now before I begin to cry. I will never, ever forget you.

God Bless Xiong and God Bless LANZHOU GLOBAL LTD.

Your ex-employee but lifelong friend.

I love you Xiong, you were more than a boss,

Bob 'Xiong' Servant

Dundee Evening Telegraph

Broughty Ferry News   30·03·07

Filed 03.04.07 by Broughty Ferry Breaking News Follow-up Squad

BROUGHTY FERRY MAN CUTS TIES WITH CHINESE FIRM

A Broughty Ferry man who recently sparked havoc in a local restaurant has announced that he is cutting all ties with the Chinese firm that sponsored the evening and had been rumoured to be considering a major financial investment in the Dundee area.

Robert Servant (62) say that, though he has had 'the time of his life' since taking a senior position with the company, Lanzhou Global Ltd, he feels it 'is in the best interests of everyone' that they go their separate ways.

'I was approached by Lanzhou a couple of weeks ago now,' said Mr Servant this afternoon during an impromptu press conference in the beer garden of The Fisherman's Public Bar, 'and they gave me a really terrific post. Basically, the company makes rubber belts and we hoped that we would see a lot of people in Dundee making the switch from leather to rubber and so on.

'It could have been a great thing for Dundee and it was exciting to be involved,' added Mr Servant, who is being unofficially represented by disgraced local lawyer Mike 'Pop' Wood. 'There was then a bit of a mix-up at the staff night out [Mr Servant was involved in an altercation that resulted in both the police and ambulance services being called to Willy's Chinese Palace in Gray Street] and I really think that it may have soiled the whole project.

'More to the point, it has come to my attention that rubber belts are not big sellers. Quite frankly, we did not get the interest that we would have hoped. I think, and I'm not just talking about rubber, people should not be so scared of trying new things. I think in ten years' time we'll all be wearing rubber belts, but that won't make me sad. In fact, it would make me happy because it would shut up the boo boys.'

Mr Servant says he is now thinking about returning to the window cleaning business, which he quit in disgust after having his ladders stolen in 1996. At the time, Mr Servant spoke in the *Evening Telegraph* of his 'certainty' that the ladders had been stolen by the travelling community. Tayside Police responded that there were no travellers in the Dundee area of that period.[41]

From: LANZHOU GLOBAL LTD
To: Bob Servant
Subject: Re: IT'S OVER

Hi How are you? I know from the start you are a clown, I laugh a lot when i read from you, you are such a joker.

From: Bob Servant
To: LANZHOU GLOBAL LTD
Subject: That's the spirit!

Hello there,
Good to hear from you. Yes, I was pulling your leg. I'm glad that you also enjoyed the whole thing. I'm just a fun guy really champ, and enjoy having a nice glass of cheap wine and getting on the old email. It's a hobby I suppose.

All the very best with the old 'Lanzhou' line. If you don't mind me saying

----

41. If needed I can confirm that this article is, yet again, a fabrication by Bob. As was the described press conference in the Fisherman's Bar.

so, I think it needs a little bit of polishing. Tell me, where are you from and do many people actually fall for this stuff?

Stay strong,

Bob Servant

From: LANZHOU GLOBAL LTD
To: Bob Servant
Subject: re: That's the spirit!

Hello Bob, Of course many people do fall for it, you know lots of gimimicks now and you make your cash. If you also have anything to tell me let me know. I am from Malaysia, tell me more about you.

From: Bob Servant
To: LANZHOU GLOBAL LTD
Subject: CHEERS

Hello there sport,
Well, you're a right little scamp with the thieving and that but I have to say I don't think you're a bad wee chap at heart.

Keep your nose clean you little tinker,

Farewell,

Bob

No Reply

9

Bobby and Benjamin are New Friends

From: Benjamin Suma
To: Bob Servant
Subject: INVESTMENT PROPOSAL WITH URGENT ATTENTION

Dear Friend,

I am Benjamin, the son of Asbenjamin, a Military General from Sierra Leone. I hope the purpose of my reason and my present situation will be understood by you. At the point of his death my father directed me with instruction to take over the transfer of the box that contains the fund amounted to 20 millions U.S. dollars.

Based on this I decided to source for a neutral person that can assist me in working on the necessary arrangement. Your assistance shall be compensated with a percentage from the fund. I wait for your reply,

Yours Faithfully,

Benjamin

From: Bob Servant
To: Benjamin Suma
Subject: INTERESTING

I like the cut of your jib.

Your Servant,

Bob Servant

From: Benjamin Suma
To: Bob Servant
Subject: Please try to read carefully and understand...

Dear Mr Bob,

Thanks for your quick response. I want to tell you that I will give you 25% of the total money for all the assistance that require of you to do for me. I will like you to let me know your satisfaction about the offer? The security company where the fund is being deposited does not know the content of the box that contain the fund they were told that the box contains family valuable items.

Regards,

Benjamin

From: Bob Servant
To: Benjamin Suma
Subject: Africa

Tell me about Africa my friend, is it as beautiful as they say?

Bob

From: Benjamin Suma
To: Bob Servant
Subject: Reply to this mail please

Well, life in Africa is not the same from country to country and from individual too. I don't really understand the motive of your question, could you be more specific? you have not also response to my mail? can i reach you on phone? I will need your contact and bank details to make things move.

I await your reply,

Benjamin

From: Bob Servant
To: Benjamin Suma
Subject: Hello

Benjamin,
I have heard many times of the African sunset, mostly from Tommy Peanuts but he's claiming to have seen it through binoculars when he was in Tenerife, which sounds a bit ridiculous to me? Oh, I want to be there with you in Africa Benjamin. Watching the sunset. Holding hands. I know, I know, I'm just a silly old woman. Why would you want to watch a sunset with me? You have your whole life ahead of you.

Bob

From: Benjamin Suma
To: Bob Servant
Subject: Reply please

I never knew you were a woman Bob. Don't say you are silly, everyone has to live as he or she pleases, this is my believe. Yes you are right there is a wonderful sunset in Africa. I will be happy to watch with you and take you to interesting sites depends on your interest. Start drawing your plans to come down! meanwhile what about the other discussion? You have your contact and bank information for me Bob?

Regards,
Benjamin

From: Bob Servant
To: Benjamin Suma
Subject: Benjamin

Benjamin,
Oh, are you teasing me? Please, are you a handsome man? Something you should know Benjamin, is that I am a very beautiful woman. For years, I have had men chasing me down the street, trying to touch my knockers and that, but I have never been interested. I want something different than the silly men here in Scotland. I want a real man, an exciting man, someone who is tough and not afraid to cry.

Bobby

From: Benjamin Suma
To: Bob Servant
Subject: Reply

Bobby,
I am not teasing, this is how i see life am glad to know that you are a beautiful woman. I am a handsome man, strong and caring, we were brought bold. I start having a feeling that we could make something good out of REAL LOVE, if it is what we call it. Could you tell me more? I love to be direct, I hate been pretending,

Benjamin

From: Bob Servant
To: Benjamin Suma
Subject: Take it easy

Benjamin,
Please, slow down. I do like you, but you are moving too fast,

Bobby

PS What are you wearing?

From: Benjamin Suma
To: Bob Servant
Subject: Reply Please

A SHIRT AND JEENS

From: Bob Servant
To: Benjamin Suma
Subject: OK

Benjamin,
It's a classic combo. Thank you, I am just trying to get a picture of you in my head. It is late now, time for me to go for my beauty sleep. Do you have this saying in Africa? "Time for the beauty sleep".

Bobby Sleep

From: Benjamin Suma
To: Bob Servant
Subject: Reply to this

Thanks i hope you have a nice rest. Here we say nice rest, I think both nice and beauty make the same!

Regards

Benjamin

From: Bob Servant
To: Benjamin Suma
Subject: Morning

Hello Benjamin,
I slept sensationally. What have you got planned for today? I'm going to nip down the shop and buy some lovely ham to try and cheer myself up. I'm feeling really sad today Benjamin, can you cheer me up? Do you know any good jokes?

Bobby

From: Benjamin Suma
To: Bob Servant
Subject: Have a nice day

Yeah, why position yourself am going to make you happy today? You will like it don't tell me you are not feeling it? You can only tell me to slow down, which I will agree because I will hate to hurt you.

Last week I overheard a true story from one guy telling his friend, the guy just wedded, but two days before the wedding he went to meet his old girlfriend, but unfortunately after the night he mistakingly exchange his pant to the girl. He got home and slept, in the morning as he went out of the room, the wife to be saw the pant and alarm! Put yourself in a position of man, if it happen to you what would you do!

pls cheers up there I have made you happy?

From: Bob Servant
To: Benjamin Suma
Subject: A Real Belter

Benjamin,
That is a wonderful joke, thank you so much, it has really cheered me up. Why did the man put on the wrong pants?! What a silly man. It really is a funny joke. And, yes, you are right, I am feeling that there is something between us. But I don't want to rush things because then it might all turn to shit.

I think I'm going to go and watch a couple of James Bond films. Are you like James Bond Benjamin? He is my dream man. I think Connery probably gets my vote. Not just because he's Scottish and not English though. If you start thinking like that you end up with no teeth like Jocky Wilson.[42]

Bobby

From: Benjamin Suma
To: Bob Servant
Subject: Hello

Darling, it happen in the night it was the lady's pant! I have am not watching Bonds these days. I love adventurous films, people like Michael Douglas, Kathleen Tuners, Devito.

From: Bob Servant
To: Benjamin Suma
Subject: Who had the pants on?

Benjamin, So who was wearing the pants? The man?

---

42. Some overdue accuracy from Bob here. Scottish former world darts champion Jocky Wilson lost his last tooth at the age of 28 due to an aversion to brushing his teeth. In a newspaper interview in the 1980s, Wilson explained this was due to his grandmother informing him as a young child that, 'the English poison the water'.

Have you seen Romancing the Stone? Douglas, Turner, Devito. The old gang back together.

Bobby

From: Benjamin Suma
To: Bob Servant
Subject: Have a Nice Day

Morning dear,
The man is the one that wear the lady's pant the lady two wears the guy pant!

Yes i have seen the romancing the stone, the jewel of the nile, ruthless people, other people's money!

cheers

From: Bob Servant
To: Benjamin Suma
Subject: Quiz

Hello Benjamin,
Yes, I am good thanks. They are all wonderful films, and extremely well acted. I think I've seen a book called Other People's Money, about some fraudster guy. I can't believe they named it after a Danny Devito film, what a bunch of fannies. Do you know who this man is? You must do?

Bobby

From: Benjamin Suma
To: Bob Servant
Subject: Have a nice day

I wouldn't know him poor me. Can you put me through?

From: Bob Servant
To: Benjamin Suma
Subject: It's Ralphie

Hello Benjamin, It's Ralphie Milne, the former Dundee United player. Do you mind when women talk about football Benjy? Whenever I try and speak to the men in the bars here about it they say that I only watch football for the legs! I can't bloody win!

Oh Benjamin, I'm very excited, my friend has just called me and asked if I want to go to a party! What should I wear? I can't decide whether to dress in something to get the boys excited or if I should wear something fun.

Bobby

From: Benjamin Suma
To: Bob Servant
Subject: The Fun one

Bobby, wear something fun! You have an excited boy here that is all you wish for! I wish you a good luck, am not going out. Yes you can talk soccer. Will be thinking of you,

Benjamin

From: Bob Servant
To: Benjamin Suma
Subject: Ooh my head!

Benjamin,
How are my dear? Aargh, my head is so sore! I drank too much wine at the party because I was so hot. The only fun outfit I had was a rabbit costume and it was absolutely roasting. Do you know any good hangover cures?

Bobby

From: Benjamin Suma
To: Bob Servant
Subject: Have a nice day

Darling,
Once a while, it is good to satisfy one like that. Please drink a lot of
water, or you top it with the same brand of drink.
I hope it really fun?

From: Bob Servant
To: Benjamin Suma
Subject: Good Idea

Thank you Benjamin, I will try that.

I have an idea, let's write a poem together. It's what lovers do in my
country, one line at a time.

I'll start –

Bobby and Benjamin are new friends...

Now you write your line! It's fun!

Bobby x

From: Benjamin Suma
To: Bob Servant
Subject: so funful!

So lovely darling. Am working on some arrangement that will surely
be of great blessing to our RELATIONSHIP! Am right about using this
word? So nice an idea, so funful, ok my first line and second line.

YES BENJAMIN AND BOBBY HAVE JUST STARTED SOMETHING
SO GREAT,

HOW SWEET WILL IT BE IF IT CAN BE BUILD WELL IN A SOLID
FOUNDATION!

From: Bob Servant
To: Benjamin Suma
Subject: Lovely stuff

Here we go you big sausage –

Even though they live in very distant nations...

Can't wait to see your new line, your others have been ok, but maybe try and make it rhyme?

Bobby x

From: Benjamin Suma
To: Bob Servant
Subject: Benjamin and Bobby poem

Bobby and Benjamin are new friends,
Yes Benjamin and Bobby have just started something so great,
How sweet will it be if it can be build well in a solid foundation!
Even though they live in very distant nations
Yes this shouldn't count since they have strong feeling...

Benjamin x

From: Bob Servant
To: Benjamin Suma
Subject: Very nice

Maybe one day they will live together in Ealing...

From: Benjamin Suma
To: Bob Servant
Subject: Benjamin and Bobby poem

Bobby and Benjamin are new friends,
Yes Benjamin and Bobby have just started something so great,
How sweet will it be if it can be build well in a solid foundation!
Even though they live in very distant nations
Yes this shouldn't count since they have strong feeling
Maybe one day they will live together in Ealing
Very possible if really they both wish.

From: Bob Servant
To: Benjamin Suma
Subject: Last bit

I wonder if Benjamin likes fish?

From: Benjamin Suma
To: Bob Servant
Subject: Benjamin and Bobby poem

Bobby and Benjamin are new friends,
Yes Benjamin and Bobby have just started something so great,
How sweet will it be if it can be build well in a solid foundation!
Even though they live in very distant nations
Yes this shouldn't count since they have strong feeling
Maybe one day they will live together in Ealing
Very possible if really they both wish
I wonder if Benjamin likes fish?
Yes he like eating fish so much this days!

From: Bob Servant
To: Benjamin Suma
Subject: Ok that'll do

OK Benjamin, that'll do us there.

Well done, what a wonderful poem. I had a great day today. My friend Carol came round to the house and we washed my car together and made it look all pretty. I have attached a photo of Carol larking about on the car. I was going to get her to take a photo of me to send you but I am too shy!! I am worried that you won't think I am beautiful.

Bobby x[43]

From: Benjamin Suma
To: Bob Servant
Subject: cheers

Whoa! Darling you have share your today joy with me! I can't wait to see your picture, i will love it don't worry. WHOM DO YOU DREAM ABOUT?

One day you will drive me, or won't you? (Bobby, i have one thing in my character I don't like people that doubt about what take their time.) I love it what is the car name? Thank you for brighting this joy. (Bobby, i have one thing in my character i dont like people that doubt on what they do).

---

43. At this point, Bob supplied a photo of a woman dancing on a car bonnet and holding a bottle of OVD rum. I contacted this woman, whose name I will certainly not reveal, and she made it quite clear that the photo was not to be used in the book. It was a moment of madness, she explained, after she got chatting to Bob in the queue at Woolworth's.

I am working on an exciting business model for us that will help our future, my dear. It will need a little investment but not so much,

Benji

From: Bob Servant
To: Benjamin Suma
Subject: Test

Benjamin,
Hello my darling, thank you for your kind words. The car is called HOTPOT. Benjamin, Carol told me that I should give you a 'gentleman's test'. It's three questions and you have to say what you would do in these situations –

1. We are in a bar and another woman comes over and asks you to kiss her or touch her knockers. What do you do?

2. I am in HOTPOT and I wipe out an entire flock of sheep because I'm doing my lipstick. What do you do?

3. I eat a lot of lovely ham and get very, very fat. What do you do?

Bobby x

From: Benjamin Suma
To: Bob Servant
Subject: Gentleman test indeed

OK my answer

I will honestly never response to any other woman kisses when am with you

I have to stand by you under any situation as long as i love you, not only when it happen in my present but even in my absent. If this happens with HOTPOT I would help you as I could.

Yes, a change in your look will never have any effect in my love for you as long as i love you.

So what about the photo?

From: Bob Servant
To: Benjamin Suma
Subject: Dreamboat

Oh Benjamin,
You are wonderful. I am so nervous about sending you my photo! I do not have the courage yet. Please, can you send your one first? That would

make me feel a lot better. I am so excited about seeing you, and showing you off to Carol and the rest of the girls! In the meantime, what is your favourite animal? I am generally lion mad but I also have a soft spot for the Australian kangaroo.

Bobby x

From: Benjamin Suma
To: Bob Servant
Subject: AM I CORRECT?

Dear,
My best animal is DOG I have one called Sharp. Am already having a feeling I can't express. I will send photo as soon as it is possible for me to do the scanning. Meanwhile, there is something that worries me. I seem to have told you much about me but you never say anything or you are not clear? You are interested in the business I mention?

Benjamin

From: Bob Servant
To: Benjamin Suma
Subject: My House

Benjamin,
I cannot wait to see the photo. I know that it will make me feel as if my heart is, quite literally, on fire. Well, what else do you want to know about me? I get upset when people are cruel to animals, or when I drop some of my lovely ham on the kitchen floor or I can't get my hair to look nice.

Talking about the old 'Badger's Lair' (hair), I am going to go to the hairdresser's at the weekend to get my hair looking nice and pretty for when I have my photo taken for sending to you. I hope you like it!

Bobby x

From: Benjamin Suma
To: Bob Servant
Subject: DO YOU BELIEVE

Bobby,
Would you be hurt if I ask this question. Are you serious with me? Do you believe in love, I mean real love BETWEEN MAN AND WOMAN? I think to love means that one might need to sacrifice? Things like money?

Benjamin

From: Bob Servant
To: Benjamin Suma
Subject: I see what you mean

Benjamin,
Yes, I believe that love means many sacrifices. God knows I found that out
with my last boyfriend. He was a nasty man that used to call me names.
He used to say that I was mental and that he wasn't my boyfriend, he was
just my next-door neighbour and that I wasn't even a woman! He was
an idiot, I'm glad he's not my boyfriend any more. He used to say 'stop
messing about Bob, you're scaring me'. He was called Frank and he was a
real hunk.

Where is your photo?

Bobby x

From: Benjamin Suma
To: Bob Servant
Subject: My Picture

Darling,
Am very sorry keeping you waiting pls tell me you are not
offended. This picture was taken by the beach. I waiting eagerly to read
from you,

Benjamin

From: Bob Servant
To: Benjamin Suma
Subject: You take me breath away

Benjamin,

You are incredible! The way you are sitting there, it's just great. You're saying, "Yes, I'm on the beach, I'm relaxed, but I'm also serious. I am sitting here and thinking about Bobby, and what she might be doing right now. I wonder how she is? I think I'll email her later and say hi. Ooh, it's hot here on the beach. Would anyone like an ice cream? I like ice cream a lot, especially the mint choc chip. I'm Benjamin, and I want to be covered in ice cream".

Those sunglasses – they make you look like a film star.

WELCOME TO THE BEACH

STARRING BENJAMIN SUMA

Do you know what I mean?

Bobby x

From: Benjamin Suma
To: Bob Servant
Subject: SO FUN

So joyful and loveable darling, thanks, you are a great imaginator!

I missed you a lot yesterday. I never seen you but you seem to have taken my whole lot of feeling! Well, we both better work hard to make it real and make happiness.

pls tell me something? Are you interested in business?

CHEERS

From: Bob Servant
To: Benjamin Suma
Subject: Question

Benjamin,

Have you ever heard of a clap-o-meter? They used to be on game shows all the time but not so much now. They're machines that measure audience applause. I wondered, would you be able to make one for me?

Bobby x

From: Benjamin Suma
To: Bob Servant
Subject: URGENT

Bobby, good day, how are you today? Yes i will surely be glad to make one if i know how to. Bobby you promised, your picture? Your thoughts please on business?

From: Bob Servant
To: Benjamin Suma
Subject: The Clap-O-Meter

Benjamin,

I was hoping you would say that. I can't wait to see what you come up with. Can you make sure it works off the same batteries as my television remote please? I buy them in boxes of fifty from Nipper Kolacz.

I have been sitting staring at your photo for hours on end – you look so mysterious in those sunglasses.

It's as if you are saying, "I'm Benjamin, and I'm a man to be reckoned with. I'm wearing sunglasses because it's sunny but also because it makes me mysterious, a bit like a cowboy. Maybe one day I'll move to the desert and be a cowboy. All day long I'll ride my horse and then go back to Bobby's house and she will have cooked me some lovely ham and potatoes and we'll eat all the ham and potatoes and then we'll go and sit down on the couch and watch The Antiques Roadshow and do each other's hair."

Was that more or less what you were thinking at the time? Oh, Benji, what are we going to do with you? You're some guy. What are you going to use the build the clap-o-meter out of interest? Maybe that boat in the photo? I'm sorry that I haven't sent you my photo. I'm just so worried that you won't think I am beautiful.

Bobby

From: Benjamin Suma
To: Bob Servant
Subject: Am waiting

Darling I promise, ask me anything and I will do. I do not know where wood will come from for the building but it will come. You must send the photo. I already love you in my mind and I will show my appreciation and build this thing for you. Believe me my good feeling for you is beyond explanations. I am waiting and then we need to talk about investment.

From: Bob Servant
To: Benjamin Suma
Subject: I'm scared

Benjamin,

I'm so nervous! Carol is coming round tomorrow to help with my make-up and hair for the photo. I hope you think I'm pretty! Good luck with the Clap-o-Meter, it should be relatively straightforward but don't be too proud to ask for help if needed. You men are so stubborn sometimes!

Bobby x

From: Benjamin Suma
To: Bob Servant
Subject: OK

Thanks darling, am relief to read your mail. I will start to build it today. Yes you are so pretty than you might think i thought of you. I am waiting for the picture.

Benjamin

From: Bob Servant
To: Benjamin Suma
Subject: Promise

Do you promise you'll think I'm pretty?

From: Benjamin Suma
To: Bob Servant
Subject: Yes I did

YES I PROMISED YOU ARE SO PRETTY DARLING

From: Bob Servant
To: Benjamin Suma
Subject: OK HERE WE GO!

Ok, well here is the photo,[44] I hope you like it! Bobby x

---

44. This man is not Bob Servant and I have not been able to ascertain his identity. I can, however, report that he's an impressive-looking gentleman, and I really don't see what Benji's problem is.

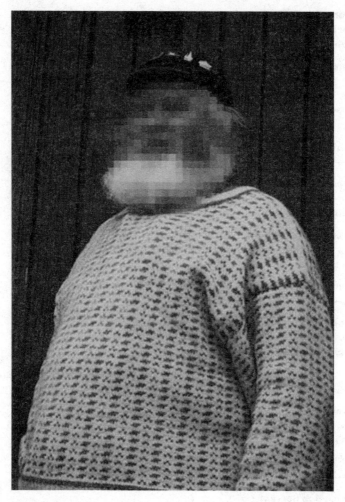

No Reply

10
Natalia and Her Grandmother

From: Natalia
To: Bob Servant
Subject: Hi

Hello! I hope that you have good day and good mood. I want to tell a little about myself now. My name is Natalia. I'm 25, I live In Russia. I hope to find the serious relations with the man in the Internet, I was disappointed by the men from Russia. They abuse much alcohol and do not respect the women.

I live with my grandmother. We have small apartment in new area of city. I want to learn about you too. I want to know, what you want new in your life? My main desire it to create amicable family and look after my grandmother. I put my picture, that you could see me, in spite of the fact that we far now.

Your friend Natalia.

From: Bob Servant
To: Natalia
Subject: Howdy

Natalia,
Nice to hear from you, and thank you for that glorious photo. Well, well, well, Natalia, where do I start? My name is, as you know, Bob Servant. I am a local business tycoon. First up was the Cheeseburger Wars which, you will probably have heard, were a very, very good time for me. Then I got hold of the Beach Avenue to Dawson Park windowcleaning round. I know what you're thinking Natalia – 'That's not a round, that's a

bloody empire'. You're spot on. It was a licence to print money Natalia. Windowcleaning money.[45]

Are you gearing up for the big one Natalia? Just a couple of days to go. I'm going Obama crazy and I don't mind admitting it,

Your Servant,

Bob Servant

From: Natalia
To: Bob Servant
Subject: Hello

Hi my new friend Bob.
Is glad to receive your new letter. You have not sent a picture yourselves, please do it. I want to tell about myself little bit more. I live in small city Samara, in the Volga region. We have beautiful river near. I work helping to the homeless people because they have no money for this purpose. I live with my grandmother. We have no telephone as our apartment is located in new area of city. I want to ask you some questions. Do you have childrens? Bob I wait from you the new letter and your picture. Yes I notice election in America. It seems a time exciting.

Natalia

From: Bob Servant
To: Natalia
Subject: Good Old Natalia

Natalia,
Thank you for your entertaining letter. It sounds to me like you and your grandmother have wonderful lives over there in Russia. You are a very lucky lady. I have attached a photo of myself that I hope you like. Would you be able to send me another one of yourself? If possible, I would prefer a photo of you in a hat. This is very important to me because there is an old Scottish poem that we use over here. You might have heard it read out by Mel Gibson in the movie BraveHat.

---

45. An edition of the *Broughty Ferry Gazette* from April 16 1990 carries an article entitled 'Broughty Man in Windowcleaning Boast'. The article reports – 'Local fast food tycoon Bob Servant claims that his new windowcleaning round is the largest in Western Europe'. 'It's so long' suggests Servant in the article, 'we have to change our watches halfway through because we lose an hour.' A representative from the Tayside Chamber of Commerce is quoted 'This isn't even the biggest windowcleaning round in Tayside. Servant is an exhibitionist'. Servant responds that the spokesman is a 'yes man' and 'has lost touch with the man in the street'.

WHY A LADY MUST WEAR A HAT

If a lady is in a Hat
Then she will not treat you like a Rat
She will not get too Fat
Or make you dress like a Cat
Or hit you with a Bat
Or make you eat a gymnastics Mat
Or set fire to your Flat
As long as she is wearing a Hat.

I look forward to seeing you in a hat,

Bob "Bob" Servant

PS Looking good for Obama. The *Broughty Ferry Gazette* have just come out for him.[46]

From: Natalia
To: Bob Servant
Subject: I'm interesting you...

Hi Bob.
How you today? I am glad, that you have found time to write. Thanks for your picture, me to like. Bob, you there is a hat, unfortunately I never carried a hat and I to not have such pictures. I am sorry Bob. I send you new picture accepted in my house. I hope, that you with pleasure find time to answer to me, as your letters bring to me pleasure.

---

46. The leader article of the *Broughty Ferry Gazette* of 3 November 2008 was entitled 'Obama is our Man(a)'.

What sports you like?

What films you prefer to look?

From sports I prefer of volleyball and aerobic. Bob, what you think of these kinds of sports?

Bob, I think, that man likes fast driving the automobile. Dear, you have the automobile?

What stamps of automobiles you prefer?

I hope, that you find time to answer my letter. I shall wait for it with pleasure.

Yours Natalia.

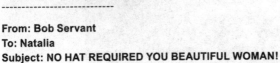

From: Bob Servant
To: Natalia
Subject: NO HAT REQUIRED YOU BEAUTIFUL WOMAN!

Natalia,
Straight off the bat, don't worry about the hat situation. After seeing your new photo I think that a hat would only ruin your beautiful face and neck. I have answered all your questions below and have added two of mine at the bottom for you to answer. Just one day till the election now Natalia and, my God, I think he's going to do it.

Bobbers

ANSWERS TO YOUR WONDERFUL QUESTIONS

Hi Bob. How you today?

I'm fine Natalia. I'm 'getting by'.

What sports you like?

I like bowling, darts, dominoes and skirt.

What films you prefer to look?

I like James Bond films and anything with a good twist or brief nudity.

From sports I prefer of volleyball and aerobic. Bob, what you think of these kinds of sports?

Natalia, I think they are shite sports.

Dear, you have the automobile?

You'd better believe it Natalia. I have a Godzilla Monkey 501, one of the biggest jeeps ever made. It is red and I need a bloody stepladder to get into it. I have attached a photo. What do you think?

What stamps of automobiles you prefer?

If I had eight apples and I ate three but then someone gave me two more then how many would I have?

Sometimes when I'm watching the TV and drinking wine I think the curtains are talking to me. Is this possible or am I just imagining it?

From: Natalia
To: Bob Servant
Subject: I'm glad to you

Dear Bob.

I am glad, that you have time to answer my letter. Each day I wait your
letter more. Bob, you to have the remarkable automobile and I think
that you look in him fine. I have never seen yet such automobiles here in
Russia. Bob, I do not understand initially your question. Concerning the
apples, I do not understand your riddle, but if I correctly to understand
you would have seven apples. It is correct? I do not know about the
curtains at all.

Yes I will be watching the election in America of television with my
grandmother but excuse me if I am wrong, but today I am afflicted with
that one of the homeless people, which I looked after, has died. He had
incurable illness. I hope, that our help brought to him pleasure. I always
dream of scientists creating medicines for incurable illnesses. As the
death of the people is a large sincere pain. I hope that the people will live
all over the world better. Now I shall go on training on sports dances after
that I shall go home.

Only yours

Natalia.

From: Bob Servant
To: Natalia
Subject: It's Obama time

Natalia,

A big 'American Howdy'!

A few hours to go! I'm excited there's no doubt about it. Whoever wins could really shake things up and I wish we were over in America to soak it all in. What I wouldn't give to be sitting behind the wheel of a Cadillac in America with you Natalia. I'm not sure if we'd be allowed to vote. I know for example that people from Fife are not allowed to vote outside Fife because they'd probably get lost on the way home.[47]

But either way we'd drive to the polling booths to meet the people and then on to a drive-in movie and then a burger bar where the girls would serve us on roller skates (I wouldn't really be looking though). By Christ, we'd have some night. I'd probably end up wearing the roller skates, being towed by you in the Cadillac, both of us with our tops off and laughing like idiots.

It's hard for me to get a real debate about the election going in Stewpot's bar. They're a bunch of halfwits and aren't taking it seriously. Frank is backing Obama because he fancies his wife and Slim Smith is supporting McCain because of how good his frozen chips are.

I'm an Obama man, no doubt about it, but I must say I thought it was a bit much that he got to do that special half hour television thingy. It struck a bit of a nerve from when I went up against Archie for the presidency of the bowling club. He had a pal at the *Broughty Ferry Gazette* and on the day of the vote they did a two page spread of him at home with his family.

It was pathetic stuff, all about how he was a family man and wanted to spread family values about the bowling club.[48] You didn't have to be a genius to see what they were saying. It was a clear dig about me and the main policies of my campaign. Especially Bob's Saucy Singles Hour (midnight on Saturdays with the floodlights off) and Wonderbra Wednesdays.

The paper even threw in a scare story that I was wanting to sell my cheeseburgers inside the club which was total bollocks. Maybe I'd have stuck a van in the car park but that would have been it. Needless to say Archie romped home and the club's not been the same since. But that's

---

47. Inhabitants of the Scottish region of Fife are free to vote anywhere in Great Britain and Northern Ireland, providing they have the needed paperwork.
48. 'I'll Bring Pride Back to Broughty Bowling' was the headline of an article in the *Broughty Ferry Gazette* of 5 July 1986. The paper's leader article that day urged the local people to choose 'old-fashioned family values' over a 'dangerous eccentric with his eye on the catering contract'.

politics Natalia, that's what it does to people. Let's hope neither candidate pulls a trick like that tonight.

Thinking of you (not in a seedy way),

Bob

PS I am so sorry to hear about the homeless man dying. Well done, though, on bravely dancing your worries away. And you're bang on the money with the apples.

From: Natalia
To: Bob Servant
Subject: My Lovely

Bob,
Today I have risen with thoughts of you also. I wish very much to join you in this talk of America. I will watch the election tonight and think of you all the time. I hope it is to be President Obama for you! My grandmother and I often speak that I would be the good wife. I dream of caring of you and to bring pleasure in your life.

I hope, what you Bob have the same sights on me. My grandmother and I talk every day. She is world to me. I shall think of you for the election tonight.

Natalia.

From: Bob Servant
To: Natalia
Subject: A historical day

Natalia,
Obama's in the White House and Frank's in the Dog House. He's got a real thing for Obama's missus and for me he completely spoilt Stewpot's Election Night Party. Stewpot put in a lot of effort too. He had a big tray of hotdogs which he would bring out from the under the bar whenever Slim Smith went to the toilet, and he was even wearing a baseball cap.

But then Obama's wife came on the screen and Frank started trying to make all these jokes. At first it was OK, it was just stuff like – she'd get my vote, or now that's what I call a candidate, or she's my First Lady. But then he started trying to do jokes around 'the ayes have it', hanging chads, and ballot boxes and Stewpot quite rightly sent him out to the car park to cool off.

Other than that, it was a momentous day and we were all very happy. Chappy said it's a bit like when Broughty Ferry Bowling club first started letting in members from Monifieth. He said for the first few years it was an apartheid system. The Monifieth boys would go and change round the back in the bramble bushes and they'd never get a slot on Saturday mornings.

But then one morning a guy from Monifieth called Ronnie Parkes walked right into the men's changing room, took out his trainers and said, "I'm changing right here". No one could believe it, but from then on everyone came to their senses and allowed the Monifieth boys full membership. I've always said that when I see a bowler, I see a bowler, I don't care where they're from and I like to think that it's only a few extremists that would disagree with me.

If only the whole world could take a leaf out of the Bowling Club's book then maybe there wouldn't be so many scraps. Tell me Natalia, did you and your grandmother have a good night together? Now that the election is over, then maybe we should cut to the chase. You know what I'm saying don't you? I like you Natalia and I'm damn sure you like me. Let's take a leaf from Obama's book shall we? Can we be together? Yes we can.

Bob

From: Natalia
To: Bob Servant
Subject: My abilities

Hi Bob!
Thank you. The election was exciting. My work is finished earlier and I, having written to you this letter, I shall prepare for a dinner for my favourite grandmother. My grandmother is sick a little and today to me to prepare a dinner like she taught me. Today I shall prepare the chinese hen and vegetable salad. Probably you Bob, love the tasty foodstuffs. We have proverb; "the way to heart of the man – passes through his stomach!" Therefore Bob, I shall reach to your heart with the help of my culinary abilities. It is a joke!!! Now I go on kitchen. I hope, my grandmother will be pleased. She is a little sick and I am scared some for her. With melancholy and ideas on you,

Natalia.

From: Bob Servant
To: Natalia
Subject: Your Granny is Hen Mad

Natalia,
This is definitely the last thing I'll say on Obama (because we need to start

seriously discussing our future) but it's great to read how importantly he's going to take the environment. That is something very close to my heart. Broughty Ferry is a beautiful place and I have always said that it should be protected. Now, the boo boys would maybe have a wee pop at me for saying that. They'd probably start talking about how I used to empty the fat tray into the harbour from the cheeseburgers van but I did that as a public service. The kids used to absolutely love the patterns that the oil made in the water. Fair enough, they got pretty upset when that swan died, but no-one ever proved the connection as far as I'm concerned.

By the way, thanks a lot for that joke. It was absolutely top class. If you keep them coming then we'll get along just fine. I hope that your meal with your grandmother went well. She sounds like a real character and I'm sure she enjoyed her Chinese hen. She bloody loves that stuff and she always has. I remember one time she was getting stuck into a massive bowl of Chinese hen and I said to her - "You're going to turn into a hen one of these days" and she looked up, with Chinese hen all over her face and said, "Fuck off Bob". But that's her all over, she's just very good fun. And she loves eating hens. I have attached a photo of a Scottish Hen, remember when he bought the bubble car?!

Bob

IMAGE REMOVED[49]

From: Natalia
To: Bob Servant
Subject: I think of you

Lovely Bob,
With pleasure has read your letter and your lovely photo. Your letter was such warm, that has kindled ice of loneliness, which by a heavy cargo laid on my heart. I love to dance and I dream that sometime I shall dance a waltz together with you. It will look so romantically. You imagine, in a black tuxedo, me in a white dress we softly addressed to each other in eyes. You would like to dance with me a waltz?

Bob, yesterday my grandmother was pleased with the dinner I to prepare. She consider that I should be the cook. It is very pleasant for me

---

49. This was a picture of Hen Broon, a member of the popular Scottish cartoon family The Broons. In a famous strip from the 1960s, Hen purchased a bubble car. The cramped nature of the vehicle and Hen's extreme height led to great confusion. Bob does not have the right to reproduce this cartoon. He produced a piece of paper from a man who drives a delivery van for the publisher, but it was badly spelt and certainly not legally enforceable.

and to see that she is not so sick today. On this optimistic note I finish the letter,

Natalia.

From: Bob Servant
To: Natalia
Subject: CHAPPY COMES UP TRUMPS AGAIN

Natalia,
A photo?! Christ, cameras in Russia must be pretty basic. I loved your waltz fantasy. I would give everything that I own to dance a waltz with you at a big fancy do full of big wigs. Imagine, my dear - you in a cocktail dress and myself in an old, ill-fitting tuxedo far too tight around my bottom that hitched half-way up my shins as I walked, and made it difficult for me to breathe.

Picture us dancing – you trying some special Russian moves you learnt at your dance class and me sweating heavily and shuffling around the place suspiciously as I cough up blood and stand with my hands on my knees, panting and swearing loudly. It would be so beautiful Natalia, a real fairy-tale ending to this whole courting business.

Oh Natalia, what's it all about? I'm so bored today I nearly watched Doctors on BBC1. I'd love to know how many people top themselves immediately after watching Doctors – I bet there's bloody hundreds. I said this the other day to Tommy Peanuts at Stewpot's and he said that this was irony, but then Chappy Williams went all angry saying that wasn't irony at all and how people are always calling stuff ironic that isn't and the two of them had a right old barney while I played the quiz machine.

After they'd calmed down we talked about what programmes we thought people might have watched before topping themselves. I said Doctors or the Jeremy Kyle Show. Tommy said Celebrity Ballroom Dancing. Chappy said Crimewatch because if the person saw themselves on it and realised that the game was up then they'd maybe just kill themselves. I thought that was pretty clever, but Chappy's not a stupid guy. He wears glasses. Any thoughts at your end?

All the best,

Bob

From: Natalia
To: Bob Servant
Subject: I'm not lonely

Hi my lovely friend Bob.
I with the large pleasure have read your letter. I hope that you do not
have problems with health and that's all right at job. My grandmother
has bad health and I do not want you, my other kindness, to suffer also.
I today have visited church and has put a candle, that you always were
accompanied with good luck. I also put candle for my grandmother. I
must go now to care for her.

Yours, Natalia.

From: Bob Servant
To: Natalia
Subject: Triple Decker

Natalia,
How's tricks badgerface? I'm sorry to hear about your grandmother. I hope
she doesn't get ill in such a way that would mean you'd have to ask me
for a few quid. Though I'm sure that won't happen. What you thinking for
dinner? I'm going to pop out for a quick couple of liveners then am tempted
to head up to Khan's for a triple decker – Shish kebab on top of Donner
kebab on top of chips. Then I cover the lot in mayonnaise and pour it down
the front of my pants while the waiters massage my bare back and sing
'Some guys have all the luck'.

Your Servant,

Bob Servant

From: Natalia
To: Bob Servant
Subject: Bob!

Greetings Bob
It sounds nice what you will do but there is a drama here now. My
grandmother is in hospital in a critical condition. The doctor gives us the
list which we should buy medicines and have told, that it should buy all
immediately. To grandmother should perform operation. And we do not
have money to perform this operation.

   Hospitals in the country poor and there not anything there, are not
present even tie up also bed-clothes. The doctor has told, that it he
helps, all than can, but it he cannot to buy it directly. If we do not buy

everything, that it he has told in time, that grandmother die. I do not know, that I then shall make, mine grandmother most the best person in my life.

I in such mad condition a condition that I seem that this dream. It cannot be. Mine grandmother can die on my eyes. We have already spent all money which we had for this purpose. Sold and incorporated everything, that were capable.

You can help us, mine are loved favourite the person, except for you at me not who is not present, you to me the closest person. I cannot leave abandon my grandmother, help me please my love. I very much strongly love you. And we required beside $450US more, and we do not know from where we can have it.

Natalia

From: Bob Servant
To: Natalia
Subject: In Your Time of Darkness Bob Servant Comes To Thee..

My Darling,
This is terrible, terrible news. Who could have seen this coming? It's a bolt from the blue Natalia, no doubt about it. Your Grandmother is a fantastic little chap. Tell her to be strong and, for all our sakes, to hang on. Because.................I AM COMING TO SAVE YOU

That's right Natalia, I'm coming to Russia! It's what Obama would want. Yes we can. Tell me what medicines your Grandmother needs asap. I know a guy called Jimmy Golac that works in the chemist in the High Street. He only works out the back, taking in deliveries, but he sells boxes

of anti-depressants to taxi drivers (and Frank) down at Stewpot's Bar for a fiver. I'm sure he will be able to sort me out.

Also, does she have enough blankets? It is VERY IMPORTANT that she is warm enough in the hospital and I should imagine that at this time of year it's fucking freezing over there. I have got three blankets and a spare duvet. It's a Superman one (I got it free with coupons from 20 boxes of Frosties back in '95) and I have attached a photo. Let me know if you want me to bring it. Maybe she'll get superpowers!

The other thing I was thinking was how am I going to get about in Russia? I am worried that if I get a bus or taxi I could be kidnapped by terrorists. I was thinking that probably the most obvious suggestion was that I could use inline roller skates? I won a pair in a tombola at the Rotary Club Dinner in 2003 before I was thrown out the Club for an attempted coup d'etat. I've never used them but I think I could pick it up OK. I've put them in the photo as well.

I am going to the travel agents this afternoon. Yours with love and the deepest concern for your failing Grandmother. Can we save Natalia's grandmother? Yes we can.

Bob Servant x x

From: Natalia
To: Bob Servant
Subject: Hello

Hello My Love Bob.
I am glad that you to want to arrive to me to Russia. But still, that to you to tell, Russia the dangerous country with terror and murder frequently to kidnap and then them not who does not find. Militiamen poorly badly work for us and allow gangsters. I see many people who are vagabonds or pumped up by drugs or that are the skinhead. These are very bad and terrible people. I ask you to think and make the correct decision well. Buying the medicine would be better and faster. It is just $450 and for a businessman like you this might be OK?

Natalia

From: Bob Servant
To: Natalia
Subject: These Colours Don't Run

Natalia,
Russia sounds really terrible. I can understand your fear for me but I would be a coward of a man if I refused to come there just because I was a

scaredy cat. I am a tough man Natalia, a real hard nut, and I am going to take those mothers down. I am also very interested in your country, ever since watching films such as Russian Roulette, The Hunt for Red October and The Italian Job. I have enclosed photos of my tools for the trip. This is what I would bring to Russia to protect both myself, you and your IMMEDIATE family. (I'm not taken a hiding for cousins.)

Your grandmother is clearly the priority. Where do you live exactly Natalia, and do I need any jabs?

Bob

From: Natalia
To: Bob Servant
Subject: Hello

Bob,
My grandmother is very sick, you must send the money for the medicine
or the doctor says she will die. You can visit later to me or I come to your
country. I have seen your country on TV and it pleases me. For now we
must have $450US for medicine. You must show you are serious.

Please quick

Natalia

From: Bob Servant
To: Natalia
Subject: Can we save Natalia's grandmother? No we can't.

Natalia,
I have some bad news on several fronts. I bumped into Cruncher
McKenzie this morning. Yes, that Cruncher McKenzie. He was walking
his Alsation (Cruncher Junior) and I had a wee chat with him about my
Russian plan. I said I was planning on going out there and that things could
get a bit hairy. He said that he didn't think it was a good idea. I told him
about the hammer, the itching powder and the penknife and he said that
he didn't think that would be enough. He said the Russians were bampots,
worse than Fifers. Now, Natalia, when Cruncher McKenzie tells you
something is dangerous, then you do well to listen.

I had a good think about it on the bus home and I have decided,
reluctantly, that I can't come to Russia and, frankly, I shouldn't let myself
get wrapped up in the whole sorry mess. I hope that you and your
grandmother get through this, I'm sure you will as you are a tough couple
of blighters. Just remember –

Hey, hey, hey, hey, hey
Ooooh baby.[50]

Yours,

Bob Servant

---

50. At this stage Bob inserted the entire lyrics to When the Going Gets Tough by
Billy Ocean. I asked if he had confirmed the reproduction rights and he insisted
that he had after meeting Billy Ocean at a butcher's in Carnoustie. I've decided to
err on the side of caution and left in only the last two lines, which don't really do
the song justice.

From: Natalia
To: Bob Servant
Subject: re: Can we save Natalia's grandmother? No we can't.

I do not believe that you are serious.

From: Bob Servant
To: Natalia
Subject: re: Can we save Natalia's grandmother? No we can't.

I share your suspicions.

NO REPLY/THE END

11
Peter's Pots

From: Peter Anderson
To: Bob Servant
Subject: REPRESENTATIVE (JOB OFFER)

Dear Beloved,
Pleasant day, I have a job offer for you. My name is Peter Anderson, I am
46 years of age and I work with UNION VENTURES INC. LTD. We
extract raw materials from Africa for clients in American geographical
region (United States and Canada).

We are looking for a representative in America and Canada to work
for us as a part time worker and are willing to Pay 10% every transaction.
These payment would come to you in your name, so all you need do
is cash it out, deduct your payment and wire the rest to us via Western
Union. But sometimes the (FBI) gets involved in case someone tries to
run with our money, I hope that is okay.

We are looking forward to your quick reply. Please if you are
interested give us your full contact details

Regards,

Peter Anderson

From: Bob Servant
To: Peter Anderson
Subject: Hello there

Peter,
This sounds very interesting indeed. And thanks for the tip-off about the
FBI. I have long suspected they are monitoring my affairs and this just
confirms it. One thing though, I'm not in America. Big Bobby comes boxing
out of the badlands of Broughty Ferry,

Your Servant,

Bob Servant

From: Peter Anderson
To: Bob Servant
Subject: HI

Good day to you,
This is OK, we also need representatives where you live. The FBI would
only be involved in our man runs with money. You are to work for us as
our part time worker and receive payments from our customers. They pay
direct into your account or send you check which you cash and deduct

your % and send to us the rest through reliable source western union money transfer. We deal in raw materials so the sums will be often large, so will your % be!

Your faithfully,

Peter Anderson.

From: Bob Servant
To: Peter Anderson
Subject: What materials Pedro? There may be a market

Hello Peter,
Good to hear from you. Can you tell me a little more please about the raw materials you deal in? I have a good friend over here – Frank Theplank - who is a trader in raw materials and I think we might be able to talk turkey.

Yours in hope,

Bob

From: Peter Anderson
To: Bob Servant
Subject: Hello Bob

HI,
Nice hearing from you. Regarding your question, Union Ventures is number one registered company in west Africa that deals on all kinds of raw materials. Still looking forward to get the informations specified, but tell us about your friend's business needs and we may be able to work with him,

Thank you.

From: Bob Servant
To: Peter Anderson
Subject: Frank's Needs

Peter
How are you my man? I'm sitting having a mug of OVD and watching Countdown. I like to call it Rum and Sums. I have just phoned Frank and told him a little bit about you. He was busy with the Coronation Street fruit machine at the Ferry Inn but he sounded quite interested and said to ask if you deal in any of the following

Timber

Rubber
China Pots

Look forward to hearing from you,

Bob

From: Peter Anderson
To: Bob Servant
Subject: Hello

Hi,
Bob i got your mail. Yes we deal in Timber, Rubber, China pots and
many others. Please tell your friend. We are a large company and so can
do discounts,

Thanks You,

Peter

From: Bob Servant
To: Peter Anderson
Subject: HE WANTS THOSE POTS

Peter,
OK, I have just called Frank. He is particularly interested in the china
pots, just as I knew he would be. Frank has the Decorations Contract for
a number of Dundee's parks and so pots play a major part in his life. If I
was to be honest with you Peter, Frank is absolutely barmy about pots. As
I suspect you might be also? Frank's going to come round here tomorrow,
would you be able to send me some photos of your pots and also how
much they cost?

It's bloody freezing here Peter, it's been snowing since last night.
What's that all about, it's nearly summer. The Courier says it's a freak
incident, though I was along at Stewpot's bar last night and the consensus
there was that it's either global warming or to do with a big fire in Whitfield
at the weekend.

It was the monthly animal noise competition at Stewpot's last night. I
don't know why I bother because, frankly, Chappy Williams has it sewn
up with his chinchilla. Anyway, I came in sixth out of ten with my rhino
which wasn't too bad. I have to say the big success of the night was
Tommy Peanuts with a new elephant impression that was really very good
and quite scary. He wore a turban to make it an Indian elephant which
everyone found very funny though I thought was a cheap trick and also
you're not supposed to have props so it was a bit out of order.

I said this to Chappy in the toilets and he said that Tommy was getting a bit big for his boots so went out and built a big nob out of snow and a traffic cone on the bonnet of Tommy's car. Then Chappy said to me, 'That's a nob fit for an elephant, eh Bob?', and we both laughed even though our hands were really cold. Sometimes he's a right idiot Chappy, but every so often he comes up with a belter. I was in stitches the whole way home and the one thing I couldn't get out of my head was, 'this is the kind of thing that would crack Peter up'. Do you find it funny?

All the very best,

Many thanks,

Bob "Pots" Servant

From: Peter Anderson
To: Bob Servant
Subject: THESE ARE SOME OF OUR COMPANY SAMPLES

Bob,
Yes what your friend Chappy did was very funny to me also. I hope your bad weather has stopped. Bob, here are some of our samples. Union Ventures are ready to offer you and Frank the best products and services. We will be proud to work with you,

Peter Anderson.

From: Bob Servant
To: Peter Anderson
Subject: LOOKING GOOD

Peter,
This all looks great. I didn't realise that your company has a partnership

with 'Pots a Plenty'. I think you and I both know that those cats are generally considered to be number one in terms of pots. I'll be honest with you Peter, as you have been with me, these pots look absolutely perfect and I think Frank is going to be quietly impressed. I am going to print out the photos and nip along to Doc Ferry's to catch him before he heads off. He always has to get home for Neighbours, does old Frank.

Peter, do you mind if I ask you to send a photo of yourself? I feel like we're friends and it would be good to know what you look like.
What are you up to tonight? I've got Frank coming round for a chicken party. We had six last time but then Frank was sick in my socks drawer so I think we're going to take it a bit easier tonight.

Look forward to seeing your photo and I will let you know what Frank thinks about the pots. I think he'll like them,

Bob

From: Peter Anderson
To: Bob Servant
Subject: Hello

Hello Bob,
This is my picture.[51] I am looking forward to hearing your order quickly so I can put my top boys onto the job and have it ready to go for you. Chicken is a big dish here also, it is a speciality of my wife!

Yours,

Peter

From: Bob Servant
To: Peter Anderson
Subject: Tall, Dark and Handsome too you lucky beggar!

Peter,
If you don't mind me saying you are a very, very handsome man. My God Peter, you're a sensation. Those are the most come to bed eyes that I have ever seen. Forget come to bed, they're run to bed!

I finally managed to track down Frank. He'd been away playing the Cops and Robbers fruit machine at the ex-serviceman's club all day. When I found him he was lying on one of the benches on the Esplanade. He didn't make much sense but he did say that he would maybe take 500 pots from you if the price is right. I didn't tell him that you're such a big spunk though, or he might keep you for himself!

-----

51. Image of an extremely dashing gentleman removed for legal reasons.

Any plans tonight? I'm just waiting for the football to come on, though some of the dross they have on the shows these days is embarrassing. Scotsport for example, that's the bloody pits. It kills me if I've not made the United game and I have to tune into that garbage to catch the highlights. Bring back Dougie Donnelly, eh?[52]

But we've got this lad at United just now Peter, called Barry Robson and that's why I can't miss the goals. He's a skinny wee ginger but, my God, the kid's got it all. The shoulder drop, the old swing of the hips. By Christ Peter, Robson could go out there in slippers and they wouldn't get near him.

Have a great night, God knows you deserve it,

Bob

From: Peter Anderson
To: Bob Servant
Subject: 500 is OK for a start

Good day Mr Bob,
I hope your team won. It is good news about the order. 500 pots would be no problem for us here and you can promise Frank that they will be put together in our best factory. We are going to give you a credit facility here at UNION VENTURES as we know that Frank is a good businessman and character. We are also going to award you a 10% discount. So all we need right now is a deposit of $20 a pot and you can pay the balance later. That is $10,000 for now.

Peter Anderson

From: Bob Servant
To: Peter Anderson
Subject: 2,000 POTS!

Peter, I just had a quick drink with Frank at Jolly's. He was having a great run on the Andy Capp fruit machine so it was hard to get his full attention but what he did say was –

'Bob, tell your man in Africa to get the guys in for a double shift because I am ready to put in an order that will blow his socks off'.

He then said, to my utter astonishment, that he need 2,000 pots by the

---

52. It should be made clear that this is purely Bob's opinion on the STV weekly show *Scotsport*. Dougie Donnelly is a long-standing employee of the BBC and, as such, is unlikely to be contractually capable of taking up Bob's suggestion. Whether he would wish to do so, however, is another matter entirely.

end of the month! He has just agreed his budget with the council for doing a major reworking of Dawson Park. They're getting rid of the tennis courts and he is going to replace it with –

'FRANK'S WORLD OF POTS'.

There are going to be 2,000 pots filled with different things. Some plants but also surprises like chocolate bars, yo-yos, jazz mags and Chinese food. Passers-by will pay £2 and put their hand in any pot they choose and see what they come up with.

It's a fantastic idea that is really going to shake things up over here. There is no doubt that this is going to take a lot of custom away from the swimming baths, the bowling club and, please God, the Limbo Walking Club who are a bunch of idiots.

It's going to be very, very interesting Peter. Certainly the swimming baths are not going to take this lying down. I wouldn't be surprised if they brought back Fancy Dress Sundays. That had them queueing right down to Youngy's Garage back when they last did it. It was a great idea and there were some wonderful scenes in the pool. I'll never forget pushing in the Queen Mother, pulling down Hitler's shorts and then dive-bombing three Michael Jacksons. There's not many people that can say they've done that down the swimming baths! I'm probably the only one.

The police made them stop holding Fancy Dress Sundays after Chappy and Frank nearly drowned. How they thought they were going to swim in a donkey outfit I have no fucking idea but that's what the whole Fancy Dress Sunday scene did to people. It sent them bloody loopy. It was just a great time in Broughty Ferry's history and I really believe that FRANK'S WORLD OF POTS could have a similar effect.

Bob

From: Peter Anderson
To: Bob Servant
Subject: LOOKING FORWARD TO HEARING FROM YOU SOONEST

Hi Bob,
I am very glad to hear from you again. I think what Frank and you are to do will be a great success and I am glad UNION VENTURES will be part of this. We will be very proud.

Regarding the order it will only take us a week as we will have the whole factory working night and day on it. The final cost to you will be $39 for each pot and then the postal costs. But as I tell you, for now you pay $20 each pot as a deposit. For 2,000 pots that's $40,000. If this is a problem we can go with the agreed deposit of $10,000.

You must pay this money through Western Union so we can start on Frank's pots.

Peter

From: Bob Servant
To: Peter Anderson
Subject: Can you come?

Peter,

Frank just called me from the dog track. He said I was to make sure that the pots are suitable for people to put their hands in without risking the hands getting stuck. Most importantly, this must include motorbike riders who have not taken their gloves off because Frank says that most of those boys are fucking nutters so if their hands got stuck then they'd be liable to smash the pot over Frank's head.

Also, Frank asked if you would like to come over here with the pots. He said that you would be able to make sure they arrived safely and that you could help install the pots in Dawson Park and stay for the launch party.

What do you think? I'm not sure where you're based (Hunksville going on your photo!) but Frank says he will pay your train fare and, if it's OK with you, you can stay in my house? I just spoke to him there at The Fort where he was playing the fruit machine. I said, 'Have you won the jackpot Frank?' and he said 'I'll win the jackpot, Bob, when these fucking pots arrive'.

Bob

From: Peter Anderson
To: Bob Servant
Subject: VERY URGENT MR BOB

Mr Bob,

To remind you we need the payment of $10,000 so we can begin. I have the factory and boys ready to go. we will need a final deposit of $40,000 for the 2,000 pots for Frank's new idea.

It is hard for me to take too much time away from work so I am not so sure that I can come with the pots. So please make sure everything is in good position and advise me when you can make a payment.

Peter

From: Bob Servant
To: Peter Anderson
Subject: Hello Peter

Peter,
You can come?! That is great news. I am very excited and so is Frank.
I just phoned him, he was driving back from the casino but he shouted
'That's great news Bob, tell Peter I can't wait to meet him and his pots but
if the pots are no good I'll shove them up his' before he got cut off by the
Tannadice tunnel.

Peter, I would like to take this opportunity to formally invite you to stay
at my house. I have attached a photo. I don't know if it's the kind of set-up
you'll be used to but the one thing I can guarantee is 'fun'.

I can't wait to see you and the pots. Peter and his magnificent pots.
Potty Peter. Peter Pots.

Bob

From: Peter Anderson
To: Bob Servant
Subject: Re: Hello Peter

Hello Bob,
I'm happy as well receiving your mail, how is your business and Frank
hope everything is good. Well OK then Bob I will come with the pots. It
is a nice offer that you have made and your house looks nice. I will come
by plane with the pots and I know the airline through business so I will
not have to buy a ticket.

Bob I advise you to send the $10,000 by Western Union or by money gramm money transfer. Here is company cashier information to use

Name: ███████████
City: Lagos
Test Qeustion: From
Answer : Bob

Thanks,
Peter Anderson.

From: Bob Servant
To: Peter Anderson
Subject: HUNKY PETER'S BIG WEEK WITH BOB AND FRANK

Hi Peter,
I'm just trying to knock out the plan for your trip here. Have a little look at it. It's only a rough draft so if there's anything you're not happy with let me know.

DAY ONE

Peter arrives. A day of relaxation where Peter is left to chill out and have naps. Bob occasionally pops into his room to see if he's OK. If he wants then Bob could massage his feet, or bring him snacks. In the evening Frank comes round to the house and they all get to know each other. We have a light dinner of fritter rolls from Maciocia's chip shop and then retire to the jacuzzi with some Ribena, a large trifle and over 400 jazz mags.

DAY TWO

Time to get 'potty'. Peter, Frank and Bob go to Dawson Park and oversee the installation of the pots. Peter checks the pots and makes sure they aren't damaged. Bob and Frank watch him closely, not because they suspect he is up to no good but because they will be admiring a man at the top of his game, doing the thing he loves. Peter then gives Bob and Frank a brief description of the pots, what they like and don't like, and the best way of looking after them. Peter then joins Frank, Bob, Chappy Williams and Tommy Peanuts for a curry at the Gullistan. Chappy to do the toast and Tommy to do the after-dinner speech as long he promises not to make fun of Bob because it's him that has set the whole thing up.

DAY THREE

Peter and Bob go on a daytrip to the Camperdown Zoo. Bob makes sandwiches, Peter to choose filling. If it's sunny we have a picnic, if it's raining we will eat the food under one of the wooden ships. We talk about parks and funny things that have happened to us in parks.

DAY FOUR

Potty Peter's Media blitz. Peter is guest on Radio Tay's breakfast show where he tells funny stories about pots and about how Bob is a good guy. He then goes into town (taxi with Bob, the two of them to go halfers on the fare) where he does interviews for the Dundee Courier and the Evening Telegraph. During the Evening Telegraph interview Peter lets slip that he has new evidence that strongly suggests a group of gypsies stole Bob's ladders in 1996.

DAY FIVE

Final preparations. Peter, Bob and Frank go up to Dawson Park, roll their sleeves up and make any last minute adjustments needed. Then some role play, with Peter pretending to be a passer-by and testing the various pots to make sure his hand doesn't get stuck in any of them. Peter to check every single pot and then to do so again wearing a glove. Bob and Frank to wait for him in the beer garden at the Taychreggan Hotel next to the park. Bob and Frank to give Peter a torch in case it gets dark before he's finished.

DAY SIX

Launch Day! Party, Party, Party. Bob to wake Peter up with a bacon roll and small glass of sherry to get him in the zone then we're off up to Dawson Park to get ready for the crowds and support Frank. When the crowds come, Bob and Peter to control the pots, checking everyone is happy and using the pots correctly. Then Frank to give a speech in which he mentions Bob and Peter and clearly notes the work that both have put in. Peter to then make a short speech including some jokes but mostly serious and talking about the pots and what they have been through to be with us in Dawson Park. Bob to then make a short speech that brings the house down.

DAY SEVEN

The blow out. Bob, Peter, Frank, Chappy and Tommy to go out on the town. Bob and Peter to wear matching denim and casual jackets and to spend most of the night together. Bob to get women over and Peter to tell them interesting stories and jokes and also to tell them that Bob is a great guy and to mention about how Bob is worth a few quid but doesn't like to talk about it.

DAY EIGHT

Peter leaves first thing for the airport with Frank driving him. Bob to come only if head not too sore.

What do you think Peter, all OK?

From: Peter Anderson
To: Bob Servant
Subject: OK apart from second last!

Hello Bob,
Yes this all looks fine and I think we will have a lot of fun as well as working hard to make success. Please speak to Frank and get the money so we can get started and make this great dream of ours a reality. There is only one problem with your plan Bob because I am married as I have told you and do not participate in women affairs thank you. Otherwise I am looking forward to hear from you soonest.

From: Bob Servant
To: Peter Anderson
Subject: Hook a brother up?

Peter,
Give me a break here. I am a single guy and am constantly looking for skirt. There are a lot of opportunities for this in Broughty Ferry, more than you'd think. There's the bowling club coffee morning on a Tuesday and the fortnightly Car Boot Sale on the Esplanade. Of course, the big one is the Limbo Walking Club's Annual Walk-Off but I picked up a lifetime ban from that lot over the whole 2002 clean-up campaign mix-up.[53]

I need a wingman Peter and I thought that you could be that guy. You're a handsome devil and I know that the birds here would think you were a right James Bond with all your foreign travel and stuff. Christ, you should have seen when Chappy Williams came back from seeing his

---

53. The *Broughty Ferry Gazette* of 27 March 2002 carried a headline of 'Limbo Walking Club Treasurer in Embezzlement Outrage' and included a suggestion from a Mr Robert Servant (48) that he had seen Hamish Instrell, the treasurer of the local Limbo Walking Club, drinking cocktails in the West Indies on a television documentary just days after the Club had reported it was in a financial crisis after poor T-shirt sales. The *Broughty Ferry Gazette* of 28 March 2002 carried a full-page apology to the Limbo Walking Club and Mr Instrell that included a report that a Mr Robert Servant (57) had in fact been watching the feature film 'Cocktail' whilst heavily inebriated and mistook one of the film's actors for Mr Instrell.

brother in Australia. The birds threw themselves at him, it was like he was Christopher Fucking Columbus when, in actual fact, he'd got the tickets free with his Hoover.

Are you up for hitting the town when you're here and we can see if our luck's in? I bet you're a confident bugger. Also, what kind of food do you like?

Thanks,

Bob

From: Peter Anderson
To: Bob Servant
Subject: OK

Bob,

If it is a party then of course I will talk to women and if it helps you out then better for all. Regarding food there is an old adage that says when in Rome you do as Romans do, as for me I like what ever that will be good for Bob.

Now please Bob, do you have the money to send by Western Union? The boys are waiting to start but I can not keep them from other jobs for long?

Peter

From: Bob Servant
To: Peter Anderson
Subject: Book

Peter,

A strange thing has happened. I got talking to this kid. He's a weird one, I used to go to his house to do his windows and I sometimes see him skulking about the pubs and so on. Anyway, turns out he's a writer and he reckons that there could be something in all this emailing that I've been doing. He's been going through it all and thinks he's going to stick the whole lot in a bloody book and get in the shops and so on.

What do you think? Sounds a bit dodgy to me,

Bob

From: Peter Anderson
To: Bob Servant
Subject: Western Union

Bob,

YOU MUST GO TO WESTERN UNION. Yes books are great things but we must concentrate on the matter in hand.

From: Bob Servant
To: Peter Anderson
Subject: It's Goodbye from Bobby Boy

Peter.

Or I could be saying Jack, or Jean, Alexandra, Colin, Joseph, Benjamin or so many, many others. My God Peter I've had some fun. It's only now, when this kid Forsyth's been here and poking through my stuff that I can see how long I've been writing to you lot. It seems like yesterday that I nearly got hold of some golden lions, but turns out I've been messing about with you boys for months and months. I can't really remember a lot of it if I'm honest with you, just that we chatted about the Ferry and Frank and the rest of the lads.

But anyway, he reckons that he has enough for the book and I should stop now for the sake of my mental health. He says he's going to take me up to Doc Ferry's and get the drinks in but I think he's one of those boys that gives it that and then suddenly his pockets are superglued after two rounds.[54]

I suppose we'll just have to see how we go. Good luck my friend, and if you see any of the rest of them tell them old Bobby Boy passes on his best. Tell them it was just a bit of fun, something to wrap up the nights. Christ only knows, the nights get long.

Sleep tight my friend, keep smiling.

Your Servant,

Bob Servant.

---

54. For the record, on that particular evening I bought Bob eight drinks, lent him £5 for a kebab and bought two pornographic magazines at his request from the Shell Garage in Broughty Ferry.

From: Peter Anderson
To: Bob Servant
Subject: LAST CHANCE

Bob,
Do you want the pots or not? I need an answer now. I will wait for an hour and then you will missed your chance.

No Reply

Acknowledgements

Thanks to David Riding and all at MBA, everyone at Birlinn, Jane Stiller, Natasha Martin, to those who generously allowed me to use their images in such absurd ways – Dennis Cox, Tony Northrup, Ansa Bulfone, Marion Boddy-Evans, Tom Nardone, Jane Tonnfeldt, Dundee United, Jayne Cremasco and Joie Leung – and to my family and my pals. And to old men in bars.

And now to Bob. I have been trying for the last week to ascertain if he wished to thank anyone and it's turned into a torturous task, which peaked in intensity yesterday. A regrettable run of events commenced in mid-morning, when Bob called, in fine form I should say, to give me three names: Tommy Peanuts, Chappy Williams and Frank The Plank (otherwise known as Frank Theplank).

'They're my best mates,' he explained, 'and they deserve everything they get.'

In the three went, only for Bob to call in the early afternoon from Broughty Ferry, absolutely furious. Chappy Williams had just played a cruel joke on him in Stewpot's Bar, swapping the salt in the shaker on Bob's table for sugar and allowing Bob to apply a typically liberal dose to his scampi and chips.

'I knew something was wrong straight away,' Bob revealed as he waited patiently at the Gray Street level crossing, 'but I kept my dignity and ate the whole lot. I was going to try and say something to Chappy about being sweet enough already but I just left it and I'm going home with my head held high. But I want him out right now, Neil, right bloody now.'

I accepted Bob's decision without question and all was quiet until dinnertime, when Bob called again. There was a distinctive echo and he disclosed that he was calling from a toilet cubicle at Doc Ferry's bar.

'Take Tommy out,' he whispered urgently, 'he just pulled away my stool as I went to sit down with a couple of birds. I looked like a fucking idiot and I've got a really sore back.'

So we were down to Frank The Plank. But, less than an hour later, Bob was on the phone again. Frank was also to be ejected, he declared, as he had just looked out of the window at Doc Ferry's and spotted Frank wearing Bob's favourite jumper on a passing bus.

'I said he could have it for a week for his birthday,' Bob told me gravely, 'but that was nearly a month ago.'

At this point I was under pressure, with the book's text needing to be submitted first thing this morning to the printer's. And so it was with some consternation that I received a stream of calls from Bob last night. I loyally noted each in turn, and here they are:

8.25 p.m. Bob calls to say that Tommy Peanuts, Chappy Williams and Frank The Plank are all to be immediately reinstated in the book's acknowledgement section after the four gather in Doc Ferry's bar and are 'getting on great guns'.

8.27 p.m. Bob calls to request Tommy Peanuts be removed from the book's acknowledgement section with immediate effect after Tommy comments twice within a minute that Bob's hair 'looks like women's hair'.

9.26 p.m. Bob calls to request Chappy Williams be removed from the book's acknowledgement section with immediate effect. Chappy told Bob that a man who entered the bar was his friend Dave and that Bob would like him and should go and say hello. When Bob approached the man and introduced himself he quickly realised that Chappy did not know the man and the man was not called Dave. Chappy had fabricated both facts for his own amusement, and also that of Tommy Peanuts and Frank The Plank.

10.36 p.m. Bob calls to request Frank The Plank be removed from the book's acknowledgement section with immediate effect. Apparently Frank is still wearing Bob's jumper. 'I knew something was up,' says Bob, 'because he's had his jacket on all night and has been sweating like something else. I caught him outside with his jacket unzipped and fanning himself with the lunch menu. The guy's a snake.'

11.10 p.m. Bob calls to request Tommy Peanuts, Chappy Williams and Frank The Plank be reinstated in the book's acknowledgement section with immediate effect after the three surprise Bob with the gift of a special chocolate cigar.

11.12 p.m. Bob calls to firmly request that Tommy Peanuts, Chappy Williams and Frank The Plank be removed from the book's acknowledgement section with immediate effect. He is phoning once again from the toilet cubicle and, in the midst of a disconcerting gagging sequence, reveals that the chocolate cigar was just a normal cigar that Tommy had placed in a used Mars Bar wrapper.

It was during this final call that Bob made a startling announcement.

'They're all bastards, Neil,' he shouted, his voice reverberating sternly amongst the tiling. 'And I want you to write that.'

'Are you sure, Bob?' I asked politely. 'That'll be the end of the book.'

'Do it,' he said, quieter and with magnificent poise, before the gagging returned and the phone died.

So there you go – that is that, the end.

They're all bastards.

Neil Forsyth, London,
July 2007